Simply Fabulous
PLYWOOD
PROJECTS

Edited by Jeanne Stauffer

HOUSE of
WHITE
BIRCHES
PUBLISHERS
SINCE 1947

Woodworking for Women™

Simply Fabulous Plywood Projects

Editor: Jeanne Stauffer
Associate Editors: Sue Reeves, Dianne Schmidt
Technical Editors: Marla Freeman, Amy Phillips
Copy Supervisor: Michelle Beck
Copy Editors: John Aycock, Kim English, Sandi Hauanio, Mary O'Donnell

Photography: Tammy Christian, Don Clark, Matthew Owen, Steven Ricks, Jackie Schaffel
Photography Stylists: Tammy Nussbaum, Tammy M. Smith

Art Director: Brad Snow
Publishing Services Manager: Brenda Gallmeyer
Graphic Arts Supervisor: Ronda Bechinski
Graphic Artist: Amy S. Lin
Production Assistants: Cheryl Kempf, Marj Morgan, Judy Neuenschwander
Traffic Coordinator: Sandra Beres
Technical Artist: John Buskirk

Publishing Director: David McKee
Book Marketing Director: Dan Fink
Sales Director: John Boggs
Editorial Director: Gary Richardson
Publishing Services Director: Brenda R. Wendling

Printed in China
First Printing: 2006
Library of Congress Control Number: 2005929968
Hardcover ISBN-10: 1-59635-058-X
Hardcover ISBN-13: 978-1-59635-058-8
Softcover ISBN-10: 1-59635-059-8
Softcover ISBN-13: 978-1-59635-059-5

Important Safety Notice: To prevent accidents, read instructions and use all safety guards on power equipment. Use appropriate personal safety equipment, including eye, ear and respiratory protection. Do not wear loose clothing when working on power equipment. Due to the variability of construction materials and skill levels, neither the staff nor the publisher of *Woodworking for Women* books assumes any responsibility for any accidents, injuries, damages or other losses incurred resulting from the material presented in this book.

WELCOME

If you think of plywood as the workhorse of the woodworking world, think again. Or better yet, just peruse the projects in this book. You'll quickly discover that plywood is not only beautiful, but very versatile.

First of all, there are more kinds of plywood than ever before. From craft plywood to cherry plywood to bendable plywood, there is plywood to fit every occasion and every look. The veneers of today are easier than ever to use, so it's a simple task to cover up the edge of a plywood board.

Of course, the edge of a plywood board, with its many layers, can also be a design element. You'll find it creatively used in this way in a picture frame and in a simple display shelf.

A few of the woodworking techniques you'll find in this book are fretwork, parquetry and even turning. The layers that make up a plywood board add a beautiful design element to a turned ring holder and small bowl.

The next time you visit your favorite lumberyard or woodworking store, don't just admire the exotic woods and the hardwoods, take a look at the plywood. Be sure you stock up because you'll want to make all the projects in this book.

Happy woodworking,

Jeanne Stauffer

CONTENTS

A temporary rolling cart will make it much easier to work around this large project.

PRODUCT NOTE

Model project was finished with stain and lacquer. If painting project, birch plywood and poplar or pine trim pieces may be used as a less expensive alternative.

PROJECT SIZE

59x22½x54¾ inches

TOOLS

- Table saw or circular saw
- Router with ⁵⁄₁₆- and ³⁄₈-inch rabbeting bits, ³⁄₈-inch round-over bit and ¼-and ¾-inch straight bits
- Router table
- Drill with ⅛-inch straight, ³⁄₈-inch countersink and #5 Vix bits
- Clamps, including corner
- Miter saw
- Jigsaw
- Dowelling jig with ⁵⁄₁₆-inch bit

SUPPLIES

- ¾-inch red oak plywood: three 4x8-foot sheets
- ¾x¾-inch red oak*: four 4-foot and four 6-foot lengths
- ¼-inch birch plywood: one 5x5-foot sheet**
- ¾x1½- inch red oak*: three 6-foot lengths
- ¾x2-inch red oak*: three 4-foot and four 6-foot lengths

- ¼-inch red oak plywood: 24x24 inches
- Wood or drywall screws: 1¼-, 1⅝- and 2-inch
- 1½-inch finish nails
- Wood glue
- Sandpaper
- ⁵⁄₁₆-inch wooden dowel pins
- ³⁄₈-inch flush plugs
- Stainable wood filler
- Stain or paint
- Lacquer (optional)
- Three pairs 2½-inch silver full-inset hinges
- Three door pulls
- Three magnetic door catches with metal plates
- Single-strength glass, cut to fit
- Glazier's points and clear acrylic caulk

* Measurements given are actual, not nominal. Standard nominal lumber will need to be ripped and/or planed to size.

** If 60-inch-wide birch plywood is not available, one 32¾x52¼-inch piece and one 23¼x52¼-inch piece may be cut for back, instead of one solid piece.

Case

CUTTING

1 Refer to cutting charts for ¾-inch red oak plywood: From sheet 1 cut two 21x54-inch pieces for sides (A). From sheet 2 cut two 20¾x55¼-inch pieces for case top/bottom (B), one 3½x55¼-inch piece for base cleat (G), and three (or four) 19½x22¼-inch pieces for shelves (V). From sheet 3 cut one 20¾x47¼-inch piece for center upright (C), one 20¾x32-inch piece for fixed shelf (F), one 21¾x57½-inch piece for top (Z), one 1½x32-inch piece for back cleat (E), two ¾x17-inch pieces for shelf supports (D) and one 18½x31¾-inch piece for lower shelf (X).

2 Using the ⁵⁄₁₆-inch rabbeting bit, rout a ³⁄₈-inch-deep rabbet across the back inside edge of each side (A).

3 Cut each of the four ¾x¾x48-inch oak boards to 43 inches for shelf standards (I). Clamp all four standards together. Referring to Fig. 1, mark placement of dadoes on shelf standards; using the ¾-inch straight bit, rout ³⁄₈-inch-deep dadoes. *Note: Use a routing jig or a straightedge and clamps to guide the router.*

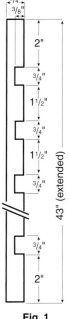

**Fig. 1
Shelf Standard (I)**

ASSEMBLY

Notes: *Refer to Fig. 2 throughout.*
Assemble case face down so face edges
are flush. Using corner clamps and
spacers, clamp pieces in place as much
as possible until they can be secured.
All attachments are made using glue
and predrilled, countersunk screws.

1 Attach the case top (B) to the sides (A) by butting it into each side flush at the top and securing through the sides with three or four 1⅝-inch screws.

2 Using the center upright (C) as a spacer, set it against the right side (A) and top (B); butt the bottom (B) into it, and secure the bottom in place through the right side. Repeat for the left side.

3 Using the fixed shelf (F) against the left side of upright C as a spacer as in the previous step, attach the top and bottom of the center upright (C) in place driving screws through the case top/bottom into the ends of the center upright.

4 While there is still easy access, attach the two ¾x17-inch shelf supports (D) to the left side (A) and the center upright (C) so the tops are 9 inches from the bottom of the sides. Attach the 1½x32-inch back cleat (E) through the side and center upright so the bottom is 10¼ inches from the case bottom and flush with the back edge of the upright and the rabbet of the side. Attach the fixed shelf (F) so there is a 17-inch opening between it and the bottom (B) and the bottom of the fixed shelf. ***Note:*** *Use of a 17-inch spacer may be helpful.*

5 Position the base cleat (G) flush with the inside edge of the back

rabbet and butted up against the bottom; attach through the sides and the top back edge of the bottom (B).

6 Check case to make sure it is square, then measure for the back from rabbet to rabbet and from the bottom of the base cleat to the very top (approximately 56x52¼ inches); cut the back (H) from the ¼-inch birch plywood, and tack it in place flush at the top. ***Note:*** *If cutting back in two pieces, splice and tack each piece on the center upright.*

7 Referring to Fig. 3, position a shelf standard (I) with the back against the left side (A), 2 inches from the top and flush against the back; attach with 1¼-inch screws driven through the standard into the case. Repeat with a second shelf standard, attaching it to the center upright to correspond with the first. Attach two more shelf standards (I) 2 inches from the top and ⅞ inch from the fronts of the side and

the center upright.

8 Measure the distance between the notches in the front and back standards and subtract ⅛ inch. From one ¾x¾x6-foot red oak board, cut two lengths to this measurement (approximately 19 inches) for shelf supports (AA) for each adjustable shelf (V). Set the remainder of the ¾-inch red oak aside for banding the lower shelf (X).

9 On each adjustable shelf (V), cut a ⅞x⅞-inch notch at each back corner, and a ½x⅞-inch notch at each front corner (Fig. 4).

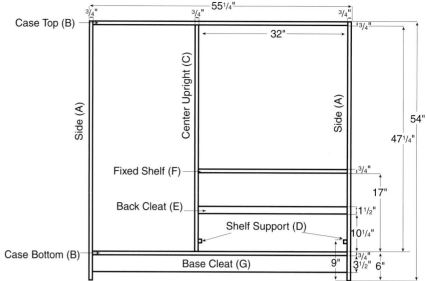

Fig. 2
Case Assembly

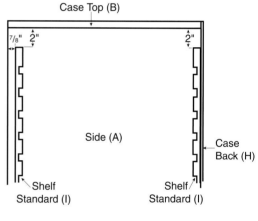

Fig. 3
Shelf Standard Placement
Side View

ASSEMBLY DIAGRAM

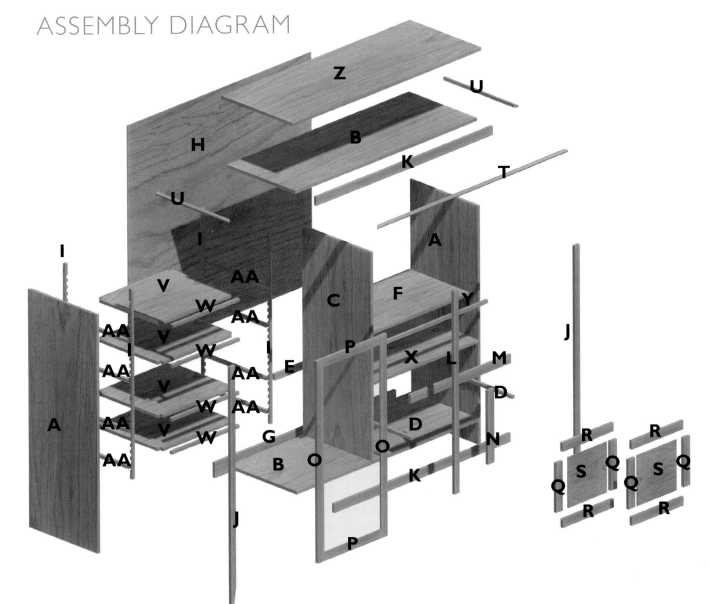

PLYWOOD PERFECT CUTTING CHART
(Actual Sizes)

P	T	W	L	#
A	¾"	21"	54"	2
B	¾"	20¾"	55¼"	2
C	¾"	20¾"	47¼"	1
D	¾"	¾"	17"	2
E	¾"	1½"	32"	1
F	¾"	20¾"	32"	1
G	¾"	3½"	55¼"	1
H	¼"	52¼"	56"	1
I	¾"	¾"	43"	4
J	¾"	1½"	54"	2
K	¾"	2"	54"	2
L	¾"	1½"	46"	1
M	¾"	2"	31"	1
N	¾"	2"	16¾"	1
O	¾"	2"	45¾"	2
P	¾"	2"	17¼"	2
Q	¾"	2"	15¾"	4
R	¾"	2"	11¼"	4
S	¼"	11¾"	12¼"	2
T	¾"	¾"	59"	1
U	¾"	¾"	22½"	2
V	¾"	19½"	22¼"	4
W	¾"	¾"	20¼"	4
X	¾"	18½"	31¾"	1
Y	¾"	¾"	31¾"	1
Z	¾"	21¾"	57½"	1
AA	¾"	¾"	19"	8

FACE FRAME

1 From the ¾x1½-inch red oak, cut two 54-inch lengths for side stiles (J). At the bottom of each side stile, measure and mark 1⅛ inches from the outside edge and 4 inches from the bottom on the inside edge. Draw a line between these two points and cut the leg taper with the jigsaw (Fig. 5). Remove saw marks with sandpaper.

2 With the taper toward the inside, attach the side stiles (J) to fronts of sides (A) so there is a ⅛-inch overhang to the outside and the stile is flush with the top and bottom of the side (A).

3 Measure the distance between the side stiles (J) at the top and the bottom; from ¾x2-inch red oak, cut two lengths to this measurement (approximately 54 inches) for top and bottom rails (K). Attach the rails so top rail is flush with the top of the case top (B), and the bottom edge of the bottom rail is 1 inch beyond the bottom of the case bottom (B).

4 Measure the distance between the top and bottom rails; from one 6-foot ¾x1½-inch red oak board, cut one center stile (L) to this measurement (approximately 46 inches). Attach center stile (L) centered over center upright (C).

5 At fixed shelf (F), measure between center rail (L) and right side stile (J); from ¾x2-inch red oak board, cut the face rail (M) to this measurement (approximately 31 inches). Attach to front of fixed shelf (F) flush with the top of the shelf.

6 From ¾x2-inch red oak, cut a 16¾-inch length for door center stile (N). Center this in the lower door opening and attach it to backs of the bottom rail (K) and face rail (M) with 1¼-inch screws (Fig. 6). *Note: Do not glue stile in place; it is made to be removable for shelf access.*

DOORS

1 From the remaining ¾x2-inch red oak stock, cut two 45¾-inch lengths for large door stiles (O) and two 17¼-inch large door rails (P). *Note: Stiles are ¼ inch less than the height of the door opening; rails are 4¼ inches less than the door opening.*

2 Also from the ¾x2-inch red oak stock, cut four 15¾-inch small door stiles (Q) and four 11¼-inch small door rails (R). *Note: Stiles are ¼ inch less than the height of the door*

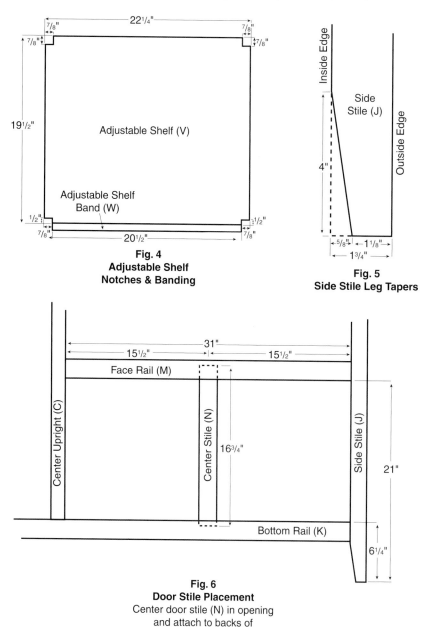

Fig. 4
Adjustable Shelf
Notches & Banding

Fig. 5
Side Stile Leg Tapers

Fig. 6
Door Stile Placement
Center door stile (N) in opening
and attach to backs of
face rail (M) and bottom rail (K).

opening; rails are 8¼ inches less than the door opening, then divided in half (for two doors.)

3 With the ¼-inch straight bit in the router and the router table fence set to cut in the center of the ¾-inch thickness of the rails and stiles, rout a ⁵⁄₁₆-inch-deep dado the full length of each small door rail (R); rout each small door stile (Q), beginning and ending 1½ inches from each end.

4 Lay out all three doors. Mark the dowel locations in the ends of each rail and the corresponding side of each stile; drill dowel holes.

5 Dry-fit doors together. Measure the opening of each of the small doors and add ½ inch to each measurement; from ¼-inch red oak plywood, cut two door panels (S) each approximately 11¾ inches (against grain) x12¼ inches (with grain). Make any adjustments necessary, then glue dowel pins in holes and assemble the door frames, sliding the panels into the small door frames before gluing the last stile. **Note:** *Do not glue the panel in place.*

6 On large door frame, rout a ⅜x⅜-inch rabbet around the back inside perimeter. Measure the rabbet-to-rabbet size and cut (or have cut) a piece of single strength glass to fit (approximately 17⅞x42⅜ inches).

BANDING

1 From one 6-foot ¾x¾-inch red oak board, cut a 4-foot length; using the ⅜-inch roundover bit, rout the top and bottom of one edge of both this 4-foot and one 6-foot length of red oak, creating a bullnose. Measure

and cut three pieces with mitered corners to band the front and sides of the top: one length mitered at both ends measuring 59 inches long-point to long-point for front band (T), and two lengths mitered at one end only measuring 22½ inches from long point to square back for side band (U).

2 Measure the front of each adjustable shelf (V) and lower shelf (X); from ¾x¾-inch red oak, cut four lengths approximately 20½ inches for adjustable shelf band (W), and one length approximately 31¾ inches for long lower shelf band (Y). **Note:** *Do not bull nose these bands.* Attach bands to front edges of respective shelves with glue and 1½-inch finish nails.

FINISHING

1 Remove door center stile (N). Fill nail holes with stainable wood filler and plug exposed screw holes with ⅜-inch plugs, making sure grains run the same direction; sand flush. Progressively sand all surfaces to be stained using up to 220-grit sandpaper.

2 Finish with stain, following the manufacturer's instructions, or paint as desired, applying multiple coats as needed to achieve desired affect. If staining, apply several coats of lacquer to seal, sanding with 220-grit sandpaper between coats.

FINAL ASSEMBLY

1 Position top (Z) flush with the back and centered side to side; attach with 1¼-inch screws driven through the top from the inside of the case.

2 Slide lower shelf (X) in place and reinstall the door center stile (N).

Hang all three doors with full-inset door hinges, using the Vix bit to center and predrill hinge holes.

3 Install door pulls and magnetic catches.

4 Install glass in large door with glazier's points and clear acrylic caulk.

5 Set adjustable shelf supports (AA) at the height desired and place adjustable shelves (V) on supports. ●

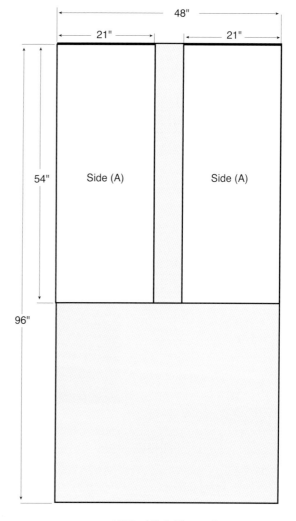

**¾" Red Oak Plywood
Cutting Chart
Sheet 1**

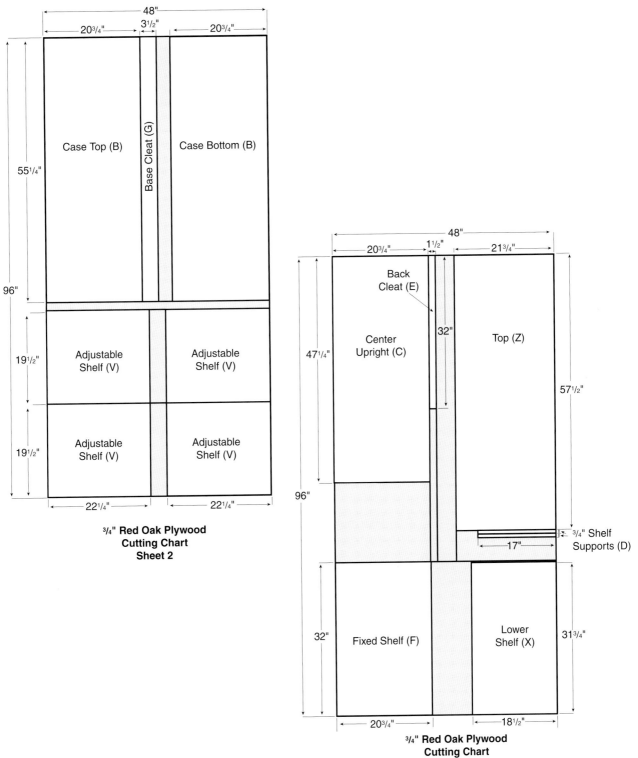

48"

20³/₄" · 3¹/₂" · 20³/₄"

Case Top (B) · Base Cleat (G) · Case Bottom (B)

55¹/₄"

96"

19¹/₂"

Adjustable Shelf (V) · Adjustable Shelf (V)

19¹/₂"

Adjustable Shelf (V) · Adjustable Shelf (V)

22¹/₄" · 22¹/₄"

³/₄" **Red Oak Plywood**
Cutting Chart
Sheet 2

48"

20³/₄" · 1¹/₂" · 21³/₄"

Back Cleat (E)

Center Upright (C)

32"

Top (Z)

47¹/₄"

57¹/₂"

96"

17" · ³/₄" Shelf Supports (D)

32"

Fixed Shelf (F) · Lower Shelf (X)

31³/₄"

20³/₄" · 18¹/₂"

³/₄" **Red Oak Plywood**
Cutting Chart
Sheet 3

ORIENTAL STORAGE NOOK

Design by Barbara Greve

Bamboo-shaped overlays accent this easy-to-build nook.

Bamboo trim

1 Transfer the bamboo pattern four times onto the ½x6-inch pine to make four trim pieces with leaf on the right side. Turn the pattern over and transfer it four more times to make four trim pieces with leaf on the left side. Cut patterns out with the scroll saw, placing each piece in order on the work surface so that the cut edge of one is against the edge from which it was cut.

2 Secure the Sand-O-Flex wheel with 180-grit sandpaper in the drill with the locking mechanism; clamp the drill into the bench vise. Make sure the vise is securely attached to the bench. Turn the drill on and lock the mechanism. Sand the face edges of each face trim piece. **Note:** *Return each piece to its place when the face edges have been sanded to the desired roundness.*

3 Mix equal parts *sage green* and *country green*; add staining medium in equal proportion to the combined colors. Apply to each piece of bamboo trim with a brush, then wipe off with paper towels; repeat until desired effect is achieved. **Note:** *Do not stain ends that attach to other pieces, or the back.* Set aside to dry.

Nook carcass
CUTTING

1 From oak plywood, cut three 10⅜x16-inch pieces for carcass top, bottom and shelf, two 10⅞x24-inch pieces for sides and one 16x24-inch piece for back, as shown in plywood cutting chart.

2 From the 1x2-inch pine, cut two 24-inch lengths for face frame sides, and three 14-inch lengths for face frame top, bottom and middle pieces.

3 Rip the laminated pine to 12¼ inches wide, then cut it to 18 inches long for cabinet top. With the classical

---

PROJECT SIZE
18x12¼x27¼ inches

TOOLS
- Scroll saw
- ⅜-inch variable-speed drill with locking mechanism
- Sand-O-Flex wheel
- #4 bench vise
- Table saw
- Variable-speed router with 1½-inch-diameter classic cove and bead bit
- Router table
- Compound miter saw
- Pocket hole jig
- Right-angle clamp
- Sander/polisher with 80-, 120- and 320-grit sandpaper
- Clamps

SUPPLIES
- ½x6-inch pine*: one 24-inch length
- ½-inch oak plywood: 48x48 inches
- 1x2-inch pine: one 8-foot length
- ¾x16-inch laminated pine*: 24 inches
- 2x3-inch pine: one 14-inch length
- DecoArt Americana Satins acrylic paint: sage green #DSA21 and country green #DSA23
- Wood glue
- 1-inch pocket hole screws
- Oak pocket hole plugs
- Wood filler
- DecoArt Americana light oak stain #AMS08
- DecoArt DuraClear satin varnish #DS21

* Measurements given are actual, not nominal. Standard nominal lumber will need to be ripped and/or planed to size.

cove and bead bit, rout the bottom sides and front of cabinet top, making several passes and removing ³⁄₁₆ to ¼ inch of stock with each pass.

4 From the 2x3-inch pine, cut four 3½-inch lengths for feet.

ASSEMBLY

Note: *Carcass assembly is done from the underside with pocket hole screws. Set the jig for 1-inch pocket holes.*

1 Glue the carcass top and bottom pieces between the sides, flush at top, bottom and front edges; clamp to secure.

2 Glue the shelf 12 inches from the tops of the sides and flush with the fronts; clamp to secure. Let dry.

3 Attach the face frame sides, top and bottom to the front of the carcass with glue and 1-inch pocket screws.

4 Attach back piece to the carcass with 1-inch pocket screws driven from the inside into the back 5¼ inches from the top and 5¼ inches from the bottom on each side.

5 Attach one foot to each bottom corner with glue and 1-inch pocket hole screws.

Note: *Face frame assembly is done with pocket hole screws from the back side of the frame. Set the jig for 1-inch pocket holes.*

6 Glue the face frame top butted into and flush with the top of the face frame sides; drive in 1-inch pocket hole screws.

7 Glue the face frame bottom butted into and flush with the bottom of face frame sides; drive in 1-inch pocket hole screws.

8 Glue the face frame middle butted into face frame sides and centered 12 inches from the carcass top; flush with top of shelf.

FINISH & FINAL ASSEMBLY

1 Spread glue on the backs and unstained edges of bamboo trim pieces; using photo as a guide, glue onto face frame sides, alternating right and left pieces as shown. Cover both sides with 24-inch-long pieces of scrap wood and clamp in place until dry.

2 Spread glue over the bottom center area of the cabinet top; attach along front and back of carcass top with 1-inch pocket screws 1 inch from each side and in the middle.

3 Fill all visible pocket holes with pocket hole plugs following the manufacturer's instructions. Fill additional areas with wood filler; let dry and sand smooth. Remove dust.

5 Working with one section at a time, apply *light oak* stain to cabinet with a brush, then wipe off with a paper towel. Repeat to achieve the desired effect. Let dry.

6 Apply two coats of varnish following manufacturer's instructions. ●

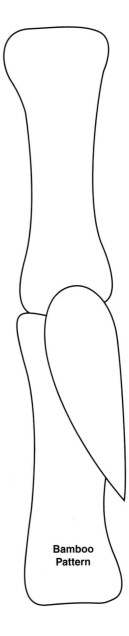

Bamboo Pattern

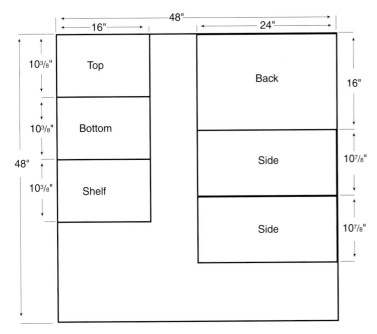

Cutting Chart

TWO-TONE SIDE TABLE

Design by Linda Van Gehuchten

Experiment with different veneers over the plywood top to change the look of this side table.

PROJECT SIZE
28¼x16x29¾ inches

TOOLS
- Table saw
- Veneer cutter or utility knife
- Small glue roller
- Plastic bag vacuum press, or two ¾x14x26-inch pieces of plywood and 4mm plastic to cover
- Clamps
- Block plane or file
- Planer
- Biscuit joiner
- Random orbit sander with 120- to 220-grit sandpaper
- Jointer
- Band saw
- Combination sander or spokeshave
- Mortising jig for drill press, or drill press with ¼-inch bit, ¼-inch chisel and mallet
- Tenoning jig
- Miter saw
- Drill with ⅛-inch bit

SUPPLIES
- ¾-inch birch plywood: 12x24 inches
- Plain maple veneer: 12x25 inches (for table bottom)
- Curly maple veneer: 12x25 inches (for top)
- Black veneer: four 1x30-inch and four 1x12-inch strips (for inlay)
- 1x6-inch cherry: one 8-foot length
- ¼-inch plywood scrap: 3x30 inches
- 3x3-inch cherry: two 6-foot lengths
- Masking tape or veneer tape
- Titebond cold press veneer glue
- 4mm plastic: two 14x30-inch pieces
- Titebond II glue (optional)
- #20 biscuits
- Titebond Original wood glue
- 1¼-inch screws
- Sanding sealer
- Moisture-resistant lacquer

PROJECT NOTES
Lay vacuum bag out on a clean, flat surface in preparation for veneering, or cover plywood pieces with plastic to be used as glue boards.

When applying glue, there should be a "smacking" sound. Be careful to spread an even layer of glue—too much will wrinkle the veneer; too little will starve the glue surface.

Tabletop
CUTTING

1 For tabletop (A), rip the ¾-inch plywood to 11¾ inches wide. Check the length and cut to 24 inches if necessary.

2 Cut the plain maple backing veneer and the curly maple top veneer to the size of the plywood tabletop (A). *Note: If the veneer splits, align and tape in place on the underside with masking tape or veneer tape along the length of the split.*

TOP & BOTTOM VENEER

1 Beginning on the bottom of the tabletop (A), spread Titebond Original glue on the plywood with a small roller. Position the plain maple veneer on the glued surface.

2 Turn tabletop (A) over and repeat gluing process for the top side, positioning the curly maple veneer on top. Hold the veneers in place with masking tape at the side edges.

3 Lay the two 14x30-inch pieces of 4mm plastic on the top and bottom of the ¾-inch veneered plywood tabletop (A). Place the tabletop in the vacuum bag following manufacturer's instructions, or clamp between the two plastic-covered, flat glue boards. Let dry for several hours, preferably overnight. **Note:** *Some glue should squeeze out over teh edge.*

4 Remove tabletop from the bag or clamps. Trim the excess veneer close to the plywood edges with a veneer cutter or utility knife, then sand flush with a small block plane or combination sander. **Note:** *Do not sand the veneered surface at this point, but spray a light coat of sealer on it and let dry to protect it from the black veneer sawdust.*

EDGE VENEER

1 Use veneer glue to glue the strips of black veneer to the ends of the tabletop (A), backing it with a strip of waste wood to hold it in place and protect the veneer from damage from the clamps. Clamp in place and let dry. Repeat with a second layer on each end.

2 Apply black veneer to the front and back edges of the tabletop in the same manner.

3 Using a sharp veneer cutter, trim black edge veneer close to the top and bottom surfaces, then finish trimming using a sharp block plane or file. **Note:** *Be careful not to mar the top or bottom surfaces.*

Option: *Using a small brush, spread Titebond II on the veneer strips and on both ends of the tabletop (A); let dry for an hour or less. (Keep the brush and a small jar of water nearby during this process. If more than an hour passes after the initial spreading of glue, use the brush and water to re-wet the glue. When it turns white, it is ready to be ironed.) With the iron set on the cotton setting, iron the veneer onto the ends of the tabletop, moving the iron back and forth progressively from one end to the other. Repeat this process for each of the two layers on all four edges of the tabletop. Trim as in step 3 of edge veneer.*

TABLETOP FRAME

1 Check the thickness of the 1x6-inch cherry. If needed, plane to ¾-inch thickness, or slightly thicker. Rip the width to 2 inches. **Note:** *Set the*

remainder of the cherry aside to make the apron.

2 From the 2-inch width, cut two pieces the length of the tabletop ends (11¾ inches) for end caps (B). Lay one end cap (B) at each end of the tabletop (A) so the ends are flush with the front and back edges of the tabletop; mark two biscuit locations on each end cap/tabletop joint. Cut the biscuit slots with the biscuit jointer set for cutting #20 biscuits. Dry-fit and adjust as necessary.

Note: *Use Titebond Original glue throughout remaining steps unless stated otherwise.*

3 Glue and clamp end caps (B) to ends of tabletop (A). Remove excess glue immediately with a damp cloth. Let dry 2 hours.

4 From the remaining 2-inch width of cherry, cut two pieces the length of the front and back edges of tabletop, including the end caps (28¼ inches) for front/back caps (C). Lay front/back caps against the front and back edges of the tabletop (A) and mark

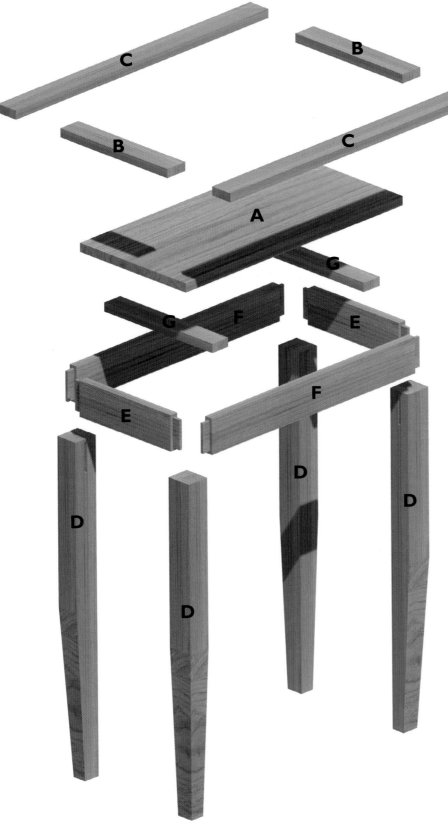

ASSEMBLY
DIAGRAM

TWO-TONED SIDE TABLE CUTTING CHART
(Actual Sizes)

P	T	W	L	#
A	¾"	11¾"	24"	1
B	¾"	2"	11¾"	2
C	¾"	2"	28¼"	2
D	2"	2¼"	29"	4
E	¾"	3"	11¾"	2
F	¾"	3"	24"	2
G	¾"	1¾"	10¼"	2

biscuit locations: one centered at each tabletop/end cap joint, and two evenly spaced along the front/back edge of the tabletop. Dry-fit and adjust as necessary.

5 Glue and clamp the front/back caps (C) to front and back edges of tabletop (A). Remove excess glue immediately with a damp cloth. Let dry.

6 Sand tabletop with the random orbit sander, beginning with 120-grit sandpaper and progressing to 220-grit, taking care to not sand through the veneer. Set aside in a protected area.

Table base
LEGS

1 Rip the ¼-inch plywood to 2 inches wide and cut it to 28 inches long. Referring to Fig. 1, make a template of the leg profile by beginning 5 inches from the top to reduce the leg width by ⅛ inch at 12, 15½, 18½, 21, 23 and 24¾ inches. On the bottom of the leg, mark ¾ inch from the outside corner. Make a gentle arc from the 24¾x1¼-inch mark to the bottom ¾-inch mark. Connect the lines and smooth out the arc, then cut and use as a template to shape the legs.

2 From the 3x3 cherry, cut four 29-inch lengths for legs (D). Then joint each leg on two sides to ensure straightness. Plane thickness of each leg to 2 inches, then rip the width to 2¼ inches. Mark the orientation of each leg: front/back, inside/outside. *Note: When shaping the leg, the outside corner will be the only one kept intact.*

3 For a test leg, rest the plywood template on the 2-inch-wide side of a 2x2¼-inch piece of scrap wood and tape the straight edge of the template

flush with the outside corner and flush with the bottom of the leg. Draw the shape of the leg. Flip the template over to the 2¼-inch side with the straight edge to the same corner; set the straight edge back ¼-inch from the corner, tape in place and draw the shape on this side of the test leg. Cut the shape of the leg with the band saw. *Note: Use masking tape to secure the waste from the first cut in place to keep the leg square for the second cut.* Examine and note adjustments to be made.

4 Following the same procedure, mark and cut each of the four legs (D). *Note: Make two pairs of legs that mirror each other: Front left and back right will be the same, and front right and back left will be the same. The 2¼-inch-wide side of the leg goes to the front or back; the 2-inch side to the ends.*

5 Finish shaping the legs with the combination sander or spokeshave. Sand to 220-grit sandpaper. Lay out the legs in their respective positions and mark 1 through 4.

6 On the two inside surfaces of each leg, lay out the mortises ⅜ inch from the outside edge and ½ inch and 2 inches down from the top.

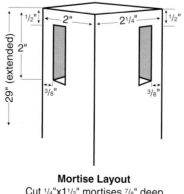

Mortise Layout
Cut ¼"x1½" mortises ⅞" deep on the two inside surfaces of each leg.

7 Using the mortising jig, cut the ¼-inch-wide mortises ⅞-inch deep at each location. *Option: If a mortising jig is not available, use a ¼-inch drill bit in a drill press to drill a ⅞-inch deep hole at the top, bottom, and middle of the*

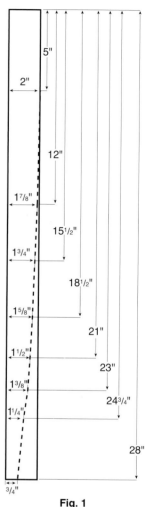

Fig. 1
Leg Template Profile

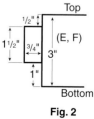

Fig. 2
Apron Tenon

mortise area, then chisel out the waste with the ¼-inch chisel.

Aprons

1 From the remaining width of 1x6 cherry from step 1 of tabletop frame, rip a 3-inch width; cut into two 11¾-inch lengths for apron sides (E) and two 24-inch lengths for apron front and back (F).

2 Raise the table-saw blade to ¼ inch. Referring to Fig. 2, use the tenoning jig to cut a ¾-inch-long tenon in a leftover piece of cherry at ½ inch and 2 inches from the top of the board. Dry-fit the tenon into the mortise of one of the legs. **Note:** *Tops should be flush and the tenon should fit snugly.*

3 When satisfied with fit, cut a tenon in each end of each apron piece (E and F). Dry-fit the apron pieces into the respective legs (D).

4 Sand legs (D) and apron pieces (E and F) progressively to 220-grit. Remove dust.

ASSEMBLE

1 Spread glue on the tenons of the apron sides (E) and insert into the mortises on the 2-inch sides of the legs (D). Clamp; remove excess glue immediately, and let dry.

2 Join the two side apron/leg units by gluing the front/back aprons (F) into the mortises on the 2¼-inch sides of the legs (D). Clamp; remove excess glue immediately and let dry.

3 Measure the inside space between the front and back aprons (F); from leftover cherry, cut two ¾x1¾-inch top cleats (G) to this measurement (10¼inches). Predrill a ⅛-inch hole 1 to

1½ inches from each end of each cleat for mounting the tabletop.

4 Using the biscuit jointer, cut slots in the inside surface of the front and back aprons centered 4 inches from each side and ⅜ inch from the top edge. Cut a corresponding slot in each end of each cleat the full 1¾-inch width.

5 Dry-fit the cleats by placing biscuits in each of the apron slots then sliding the cleat over the biscuit. The flat top of the cleat should be flush with the top edge of the front and back aprons. Adjust if necessary then glue in place. Remove excess glue immediately.

6 Place the curly maple side of the tabletop (A) down on the work surface. Center the base upside down on the tabletop and secure with 1¼-inch screws driven through

the predrilled cleat holes and into the bottom of the tabletop.

FINISH

1 Set table upright. Using a damp rag, go over the entire table base to check for glue marks, which will show up as lighter areas. Remove glue marks with a cabinet scraper or by sanding, remembering to always sand with the grain. Since the water will raise the grain slightly, finish-sand the base with 220-grit sandpaper.

Note: *Project may be stained as desired before finishing.*

2 Apply two coats of sanding sealer, then two coats of moisture-resistant lacquer following manufacturer's instructions. ●

SWEET JELLY CABINET

Design by Loretta Mateik

Tall and narrow, this cabinet fits anywhere and can hold jars of preserves, balls of yarn or extra towels.

CUTTING

1 From the ¾-inch oak plywood, cut one 15x8¼-inch piece for top (L), two 7x44-inch pieces for sides (D), four 7x11¾-inch pieces for shelves (E), two 2½x44-inch pieces for front stiles (A), two 2½x8³⁄₁₆-inch pieces for front rails (B), one 7¹¹⁄₁₆x34½-inch piece for door (F) and two 1½x11-inch pieces for front face braces (C).

2 From the ⅛-inch birch plywood, cut one 12¾x38½-inch piece for back (O).

3 Plane (or have planed) the Brazilian cherry to ¾-inch thickness, then rip it into ¼-inch strips for trim pieces (G, H, I, J, K, M and N). **Note:** *Make six passes, enough for at least 22 feet.*

4 Transfer the side cutout pattern onto the bottom of one side (D). Clamp both sides (D) together and cut both at the same time using the scroll saw.

5 Sand all faces of all pieces and remove any saw marks, then wipe clean.

6 From the ¼x¾-inch Brazilian cherry, cut two 44-inch pieces with square cuts on both ends for the front side edges (G).

7 From ¼x¾-inch strips of Brazilian cherry, cut trim pieces with mitered ends as follows: one 8³⁄₁₆-inch bottom rail trim piece (H), two 3¾-inch bottom stile trim pieces (I), two 35-inch door side trim pieces (J), two 8³⁄₁₆-inch door end top/bottom pieces (K) and one 15½-inch top front trim piece (M). **Note:** *The bottom face stile and rail trim pieces will be inside corners and all the rest will be outside corners.*

8 From ¼x¾-inch strips of Brazilian cherry, cut two 8½-inch pieces for top side trim pieces (N), mitering the front end only of each piece.

ASSEMBLE & FINISH

1 Set the two front stiles (A) face down on the work surface. Spread glue on the front rails (B) and set them between the stiles, with top rail flush at the top and bottom rail beginning 3¾ inches from the bottom. Clamp in place. Glue and center the front face braces (C) side to side on the backs of the

---

PROJECT SIZE
15½x8½x44⅝ inches

TOOLS
- Table saw
- Planer
- Clamps
- Scroll saw
- Palm sander
- Miter saw
- Carpenter's square
- Brad nailer with ⅝- and 1⅛-inch brads
- Drill

SUPPLIES
- ¾-inch oak plywood: 48x48 inches
- ⅛-inch birch plywood: 18x48 inches
- ⅞x8-inch Brazilian cherry*: 48 inches
- Sandpaper
- Wood glue
- Wood putty to match wood
- DecoArt Americana satin varnish #DS15
- Door hardware: hinges, knob and magnetic catch

* Measurements given are actual, not nominal. Standard nominal lumber will need to be ripped and/or planed to size.

(E), then, with the top of each shelf at each line, nail through the side (D) into the ends of each shelf (E) with 1⅛-inch brads.

3 Attach face frame to the front of the case with glue and 1⅛-inch nails through the face into the edges of the sides and the shelves. Remove excess glue immediately. Check to make sure box is square, then clamp and let dry.

4 Attach trim pieces (G, H, I, J, K, M and N) with glue and ⅝-inch brads.

5 Fill all nail holes with wood putty to match wood.

6 Rough-fit the door into the face frame. Trim if necessary, leaving

P	T	W	L	#
SWEET JELLY CABINET CUTTING CHART (Actual Sizes)				
A	¾"	2½"	44"	2
B	¾"	2½"	8³⁄₁₆"	2
C	¾"	1½"	11"	2
D	¾"	7"	44"	2
E	¾"	7"	11¾"	4
F	¾"	7¹¹⁄₁₆"	34½"	1
G	¼"	¾"	44"	2
H	¼"	¾"	8³⁄₁₆"	1
I	¼"	¾"	3¾"	2
J	¼"	¾"	35"	2
K	¼"	¾"	8³⁄₁₆"	2
L	¾"	15"	8¼"	1
M	¼"	¾"	15½"	1
N	¼"	¾"	8½"	2
O	⅛"	12¾"	38½"	1

ls, overlapping onto the stiles so the per brace and rail are flush with the), and the bottom brace and rail are sh at the bottom of the rail. Secure h 1⅛-inch brads through the brace and into the stiles and rails. Remove e runs; let dry.

2 Lay out the sides (D) with inside surface facing up, back to back, and tops and bottoms flush. Measuring from the bottom, mark 6, 15¼, 24¼ and 33¼ inches (see Fig. 1). Using a carpenter's square, draw a line across both boards at each mark. Spread glue on the 7-inch edges of each shelf

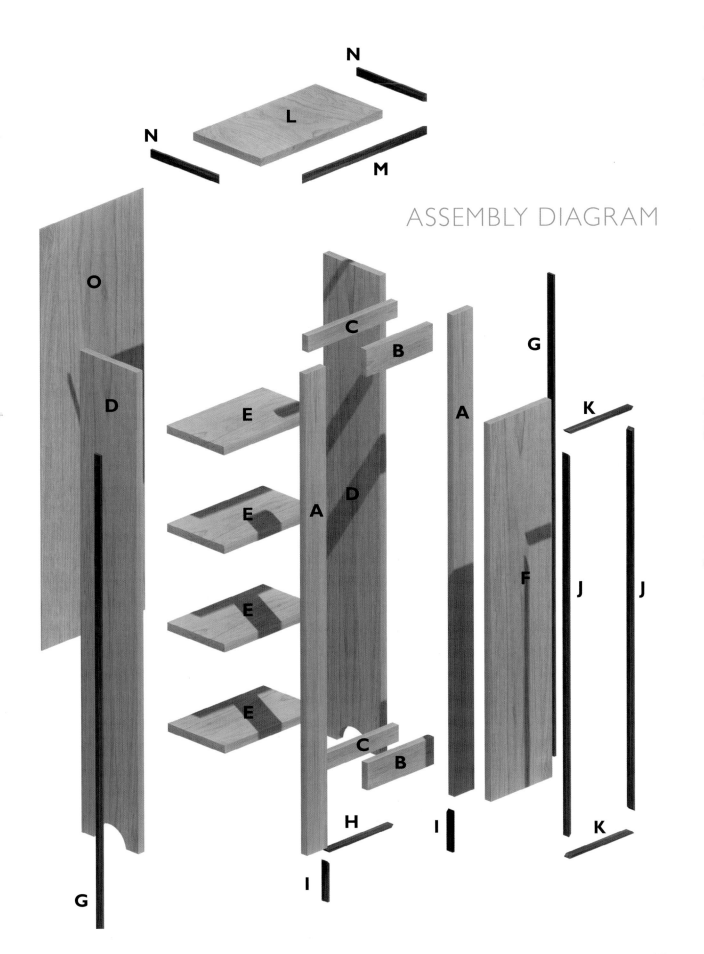

ASSEMBLY DIAGRAM

a ⅟16-inch space around the door perimeter for clearance.

7 Using glue and 1⅛-inch brads, attach top (L) to cabinet with backs flush. Set nails and putty holes; let dry. Sand smooth. Wipe clean.

8 Apply several coats of varnish to inside and outside of cabinet, and inside face of back; let dry. Attach back using ⅝-inch brads, then varnish the outside of the back.

9 Attach door to cabinet with hinges, drilling pilot holes for screws. Attach doorknob and magnetic catch. ●

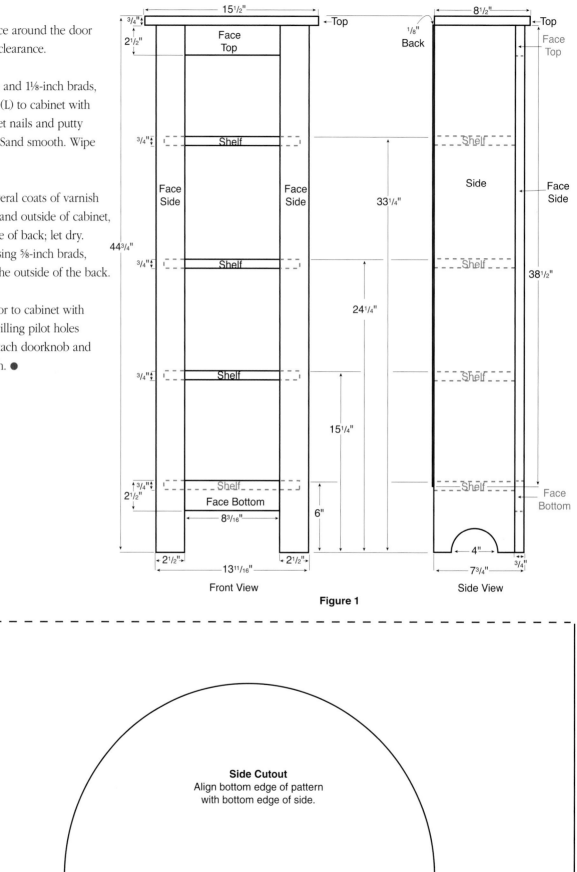

Figure 1

Side Cutout
Align bottom edge of pattern
with bottom edge of side.

HANDY RACK

Design by Barbara Greve

Hang hand towels near the sink in a kitchen or bath, or hang mini quilts in the family room.

CUTTING

1 From the ½-inch plywood rip and cut two 7x12-inch pieces for sides, one 7x21½-inch piece for top and one 6x20½-inch piece for shelf.

2 Transfer the side curve pattern onto one of the sides; clamp both sides together and cut the curve on both at the same time using the jigsaw.

3 With sides still clamped together, measure 1⅜ inches from the front and 1⅜ inches from the bottom. On the drill press, drill a ¾-inch-diameter hole centered at this mark through both side pieces. Unclamp the sides.

4 With the pocket hole jig, drill two holes on the inside surface of each side to attach the top, and two at each end of the shelf bottom to attach the sides.

5 Sand surfaces smooth, removing saw marks on curves; wipe clean.

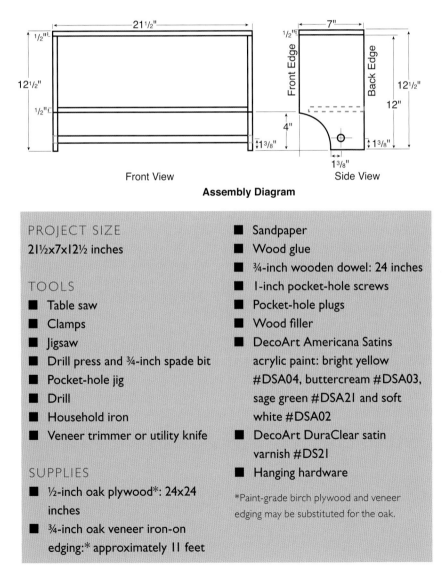

Front View

Side View

Assembly Diagram

PROJECT SIZE
21½x7x12½ inches

TOOLS
- Table saw
- Clamps
- Jigsaw
- Drill press and ¾-inch spade bit
- Pocket-hole jig
- Drill
- Household iron
- Veneer trimmer or utility knife

SUPPLIES
- ½-inch oak plywood*: 24x24 inches
- ¾-inch oak veneer iron-on edging:* approximately 11 feet

- Sandpaper
- Wood glue
- ¾-inch wooden dowel: 24 inches
- 1-inch pocket-hole screws
- Pocket-hole plugs
- Wood filler
- DecoArt Americana Satins acrylic paint: bright yellow #DSA04, buttercream #DSA03, sage green #DSA21 and soft white #DSA02
- DecoArt DuraClear satin varnish #DS21
- Hanging hardware

*Paint-grade birch plywood and veneer edging may be substituted for the oak.

ASSEMBLE & FINISH

1 Iron on veneer edging to all exposed plywood edges. Trim excess.

2 Spread a layer of glue on the ends of the shelf, and around the holes in the sides. *Note: Dowel needs to be cut to 21½ inches or trimmed flush after it's glued.* Slide sides over each end of the dowel, then clamp the shelf in place so the top of the shelf is 7½ inches from the top of the sides. Attach shelf with 1-inch pocket screws.

3 Spread glue on the tops of the sides, then clamp the top in place flush with the outside edges of the sides; attach with 1-inch pocket hole screws.

4 Glue the pocket hole plugs in place in the sides. Remove excess glue; let dry.

5 Fill nail holes and gaps with wood filler. Let dry, then sand smooth and remove dust.

6 Mix equal amounts of *bright yellow* and *buttercream*. Apply two coats to the dowel rod, shelf and top, letting dry and sanding lightly with 320-grit sandpaper between coats. Let dry.

7 Mix equal amounts of *sage green* and *soft white*. Apply two coats to sides, letting dry and sanding as in step 6. Let dry.

8 Finish with a coat of satin varnish following manufacturer's instructions.

9 Attach hanging hardware to back of top. ●

Side Curve Pattern

Bottom Edge

Front Edge

CORNER CURIO SHELF

Design by Barbara Greve

Dress up an unadorned corner with a display of your favorite tiny treasures.

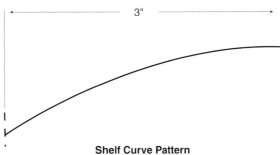

Shelf Curve Pattern

CUTTING

1 From the ½-inch plywood, rip and cut one 9x22-inch piece for first side, one 9½x22-inch piece for second side, one 8x8-inch piece and one 5x5-inch piece.

2 For shelves, cut the 5-inch square and the 8-inch square in half diagonally. From one of the 5-inch halves, cut a smaller triangle with 2½-inch sides.

3 On one 9x22-inch side piece, draw vertical lines 3 inches apart. Referring to the cutting diagram, mark 9¾ inches from the bottom at the front edge, and 16¾ inches from the bottom at the first 3-inch line. Mark the 9½x22-inch side piece in similar manner, beginning with the 3-inch vertical lines ½ inch from the back edge.

4 Transfer the curve pattern to each side as shown in the cutting diagram. With the front edges of the two sides together, clamp in place and cut the side profile on both sides at the same time using the jigsaw.

5 Sand rough edges smooth and remove dust.

6 Drill three pocket holes at the top, center and bottom along the back edge of the 9-inch side for attaching the second side. Drill one pocket hole in each side on the bottom of the 5-inch and both 8-inch shelves.

ASSEMBLE & FINISH

1 Iron on the veneer edging to the front edges of the four shelves, and to the front edges, curves, and bottom of each side. Trim off excess.

2 Spread glue on the back edge of the 9-inch side. Butt it into the 9½-inch side and hold in place with a

PROJECT SIZE
13⅜x7x22 inches

TOOLS
- Table saw
- Clamps, including right-angle
- Jigsaw
- Sander with 120- to 320-grit sandpaper
- Pocket hole jig
- Variable speed drill with ³/₃₂-inch bit
- Veneer trimmer or utility knife
- Household iron

SUPPLIES
- ½-inch plywood: one 12x48-inch piece and one 12x24-inch piece
- ¾-inch birch veneer iron-on edging: approximately 10 feet
- Stainable wood glue
- 1-inch pocket hole screws
- #4x¾-inch wood screws
- DecoArt Americana water-based stain: chestnut #AMS03
- DecoArt DuraClear satin varnish #DS21

right-angle clamp. Attach with 1-inch pocket hole screws. Remove excess glue immediately; let dry.

3 Referring to the shelf placement diagram, measure and mark ½, 7¼, 14 and 19⁹⁄₁₆ inches from the bottom for the bottom of each shelf. Apply glue to the back edges of each of the bottom three shelves and attach with pocket hole screws. For the top shelf, predrill and slightly countersink holes, then attach by driving wood screws through the sides into the ends of the shelf. Remove excess glue immediately; let dry.

4 Apply stain, then satin varnish following the manufacturer's instructions. ●

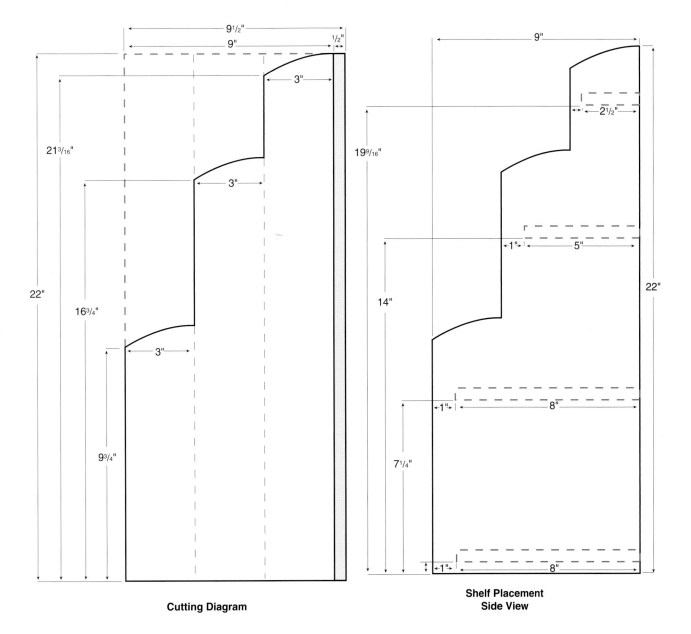

Cutting Diagram

**Shelf Placement
Side View**

MESSAGE & MAIL CENTER

Design by Patti J. Ryan

Handy organizer features both cork and chalk boards and is generously sized to hold envelopes and small packages.

CUTTING

Note: *Refer to Cutting Diagram on page 36.*

1 From the ½-inch plywood, cut two 12x20-inch pieces for front and back, one 6x12-inch piece for top, one 7½x12-inch piece for bottom, and two 5¼x12-inch pieces for shelves. Mark inside, outside, top and bottom of each piece.

PROJECT SIZE
13⅜x7⅞x23⅜ inches

TOOLS
- Table saw
- Router with ½-inch straight bit
- Mallet
- Belt-style clamp
- Drill
- Miter saw
- Nail set
- Household iron

SUPPLIES
- ½-inch birch plywood: 24x48 inches
- 3-inch-wide chair rail: 3 feet
- ¾-inch half-round: 3 feet
- Shoe molding: 4 feet
- ⅜-inch decorative molding: 1 foot
- Sandpaper: 80- and 220-grit
- Masking tape
- Krylon primer: white #1315
- Krylon chalkboard paint: black #807
- Wood glue
- #6x¾-inch screws
- Stainable wood filler
- Finish nails: ¾- and 1-inch
- ½-inch brads
- ½-inch-wide birch iron-on veneer edge tape: 9 feet
- Cork sheeting: 12x12 inches
- Krylon spray adhesive #7010
- DecoArt Americana Satins: soft natural #DSA40; staining medium #DSA432; varnish #DSA28 and stain conditioner #DSA33.
- Two D-ring-style hangers with screws

2 With the insides facing up, place the front and back pieces together with the 20-inch edges next to each other and top edges flush; measure and mark 4, 4½, 9 and 9½ inches from the top. Flip boards to the outside; measure and mark matching lines for screw placement. Using the carpenter's square, draw a line across both boards at each mark. Flip boards back to the inside surface. Rout a ⅛-inch-deep, ½-inch-wide dado inside across both boards between each set of marks (Fig. 1).

3 Lightly sand all pieces to remove rough edges; wipe clean.

CHALKBOARD

1 On the outside of the front piece, mask off all but the lower 10½ inches using masking tape and newspaper.

2 Following manufacturer's instructions, apply one to two coats of primer, then two to three coats of chalkboard paint. Remove protective newspaper.

CASE ASSEMBLY

1 Dry-fit the shelves in the dadoes. Adjust as necessary so front and back edges of shelves are flush with the sides of the front and back; disassemble. Spread a fine bead of glue in the dadoes and reassemble, tapping shelves into dadoes with mallet if necessary; secure with belt clamp.

2 Drill and countersink two screw holes through front and back into each end of each shelf; secure shelves with two ¾-inch screws.

3 Remove belt clamp and wipe away any excess glue with a damp cloth.

4 Place top board flush with all outside edges of front and back; attach with glue and two or three ¾-inch screws predrilled and countersunk through the top and into the top edges of the front and back.

5 Place the bottom board flush with sides and the outside edge of the back; attach with two or three ¾-inch screws predrilled and countersunk through the bottom and into the bottom edges of the front and back.

6 Fill all screw holes with wood filler; let dry. Sand flush with the sanding block; remove dust.

TRIM

1 Cut chair rail with mitered corners to fit around the front and sides of the top. Predrill holes and glue to top flush with the bottom of the top; secure with ¾- or 1-inch finish nails; set nails.

2 Cut the half-round molding with mitered corners to fit around the front and sides of the bottom piece, with bottom edges flush. *Note: This creates a lip and defines the chalk holder.* Attach with glue and brads; set the brads.

3 Apply iron-on veneer edge tape to exposed plywood edges, doing edges of front and back first, then shelves. Trim edging to fit.

4 Cut two pieces of shoe molding to fit on each side of front piece with outside edges flush; glue and brad-nail in place; set the brads.

5 Cut the cork to fit between the pieces of shoe molding and between the chair rail and the chalkboard on the front. Use newspaper to protect the moldings and chalkboard from overspray; spray adhesive onto the front of the message center and the back of the cork. Remove the masking from the moldings/chalkboard. Let adhesive set up for a moment, then smooth the cork in place. Apply a light weight to the area while the adhesive dries.

6 Cut a piece of the ⅜-inch molding to fit between the shoe moldings over the cork/chalkboard seam; attach with glue and brad nails. Set the brads.

7 Fill nail/brad holes and gaps in miters with wood filler; let dry, then sand smooth. Remove dust.

FINISH

1 Apply a coat of stain conditioner to all wood surfaces; sand lightly with 220-grit sandpaper and remove dust.

2 Mix equal amounts of *soft natural* and staining medium. *Note: Mix enough to cover the wood surfaces of the message center twice.* Apply mixture with a brush to wood surfaces, using long strokes; let set five or 10 minutes, then wipe off. Let dry 30 minutes. Apply a second coat; let dry.

3 Apply a coat of satin varnish following manufacturer's directions.

4 Install D-rings to top edge of back with screws. ●

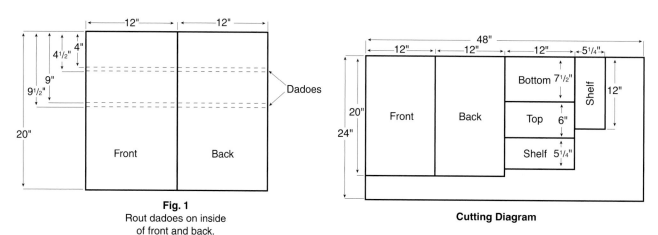

Fig. 1
Rout dadoes on inside
of front and back.

Cutting Diagram

PETITE PIE CABINET

Design by Loretta Matiek

Your fresh-baked treats can safely cool behind a screened door where they are protected from hungry pie-snatchers.

CUTTING

1 From the ⅝-inch plywood, cut one 13¾x13-inch piece for top (D), one 12x34½-inch piece for door (H), three 11¼x11-inch pieces for shelves (B), two 11½x34½-inch pieces for sides (A) and one 14x13-inch piece for base (E). Mark each side piece "top" and "inside" for reference.

2 From the ½-inch plywood, cut one 11¼x34½-inch piece for back (C). Mark this for "top" and "inside" as for the sides.

3 Lay out the sides (A) butted together back edge to back edge with the tops in the same direction and the inside surface facing up. With the straightedge or carpenter's square mark across both boards 8, 16¾ and 25 inches from the side bottoms for placement of shelves. (Fig. 1)

4 Using a router with the ⅝-inch straight bit and a straightedge clamped in place as a guide, rout ¼-inch-deep dadoes across both side pieces (A) at the same time, with the cut

to the top side of each line. **Note:** *Make two passes with the router, cutting ⅛ inch deep each time.*

5 Reposition guide to cut ½ inch from the back edge of each side (A); cut a ¼-inch-deep rabbet, making two ⅛-inch passes.

6 Mark the center cutout section of the door panel so the frame is 1½ inches wide on the sides and 2 inches wide at the top and bottom. Position the door panel on the table saw deck, then raise the blade through the plywood until the blade is just visible. Cut each side to within 6 inches of the corner. **Note:** *Cut the sides, then reset the fence to cut the top and bottom.* Finish cutting out the center of the door panel with a scroll saw or jigsaw.

7 Sand off all saw marks and sand all surfaces smooth.

ASSEMBLE

1 Slide the shelves (B) into the dadoes in the sides (A) and set the back (C) in place in the rabbet. Check fit. Glue and secure with 1⅛-inch brads through the sides into the ends of the shelves. Make sure case is square, then nail through the back into the rabbets.

PROJECT SIZE
15¼x13¾x35¾ inches

TOOLS
- Table saw
- Carpenter's square or straightedge
- Router with edge guide and ⅝-inch straight bit
- Scroll saw or jigsaw
- Palm sander
- Brad nailer with ⅝- and 1⅛-inch brads
- Stapler with ¼-inch staples
- Drill with 5/32- and ⅛-inch bits

SUPPLIES
- ⅝-inch birch plywood: 48x48 inches
- ½-inch birch plywood: 12x36 inches
- ⅜x¾-inch embossed molding: 48 inches
- ⅝-inch rope molding: 96 inches
- Wood glue
- Wood putty
- DecoArt Americana acrylic paints: toffee #DA059, mocha #DA060, terra cotta #DA062 and burnt sienna #DA063
- Aluminum screen: 12x36 inches
- Two hinges
- ⅛-inch wooden dowel: ¾ inch
- One ¾-inch wooden knob
- One magnetic catch
- DecoArt Americana satin varnish #DS15

ASSEMBLY DIAGRAM

PETITE PIE CABINET CUTTING CHART
(Actual Sizes)

P	T	W	L	#
A	5/8"	11½"	34½"	2
B	5/8"	11"	11¼"	3
C	½"	11¼"	34½"	1
D	5/8"	13¾"	13"	1
E	5/8"	14"	13"	1
F	3/8"	¾"	15¼"	1
G	3/8"	¾"	13¾"	2
H	5/8"	12"	34½"	1
I	3/8"	5/8"	10¼"	2
J	3/8"	5/8"	31¾"	2

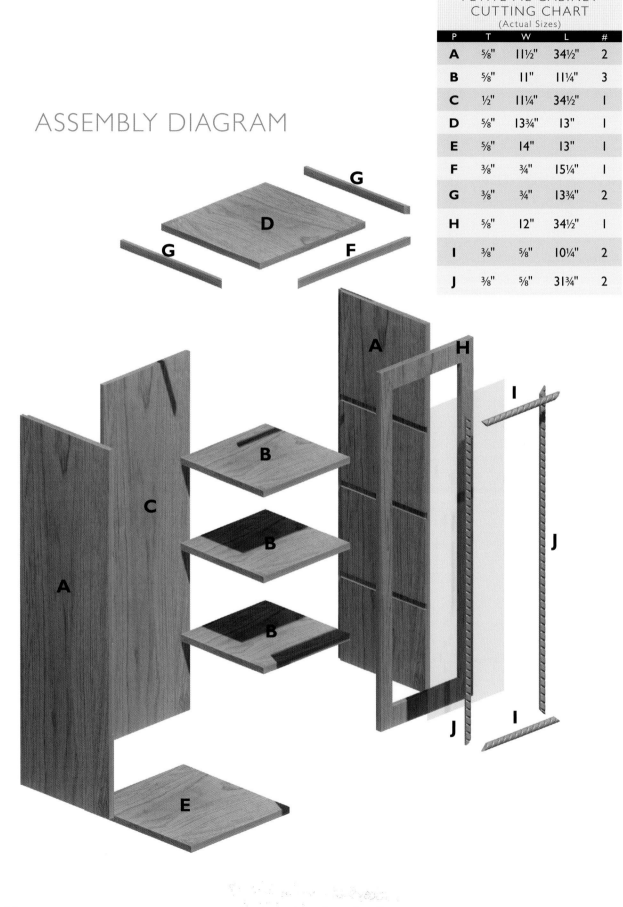

2 Attach the top (D) with glue and 1⅛-inch brads equally spaced over the sides and flush at the back.

3 Attach the bottom (E) in the same manner as the top.

4 Cut the embossed molding (F and G) to wrap the top face and side edges, mitering the corners. Attach with glue and ⅝-inch brads.

5 Set nails; fill all nail holes and any voids or gaps in the plywood.

6 Cut the rope molding to fit around the door center, mitering the corners (I and J).

FINISH

Note: *Apply two coats, letting dry and sanding lightly after each coat.*

1 Base-coat cabinet as follows:
Outside of top, back, sides and door—*terra cotta.*
Inside cabinet—Mix one part *mocha* and one part *toffee.*
Rope trim, base and knob—*burnt sienna.*

2 Dry-fit door (H) to assure proper opening. Trim to fit and touch up finish as needed.

3 Staple the screen over door opening on the outside of the door using ¼-inch staples, then trim edges. **Note:** *Trim screen close enough for the rope molding to sufficiently cover the screen edges, but not so short that it would pull through the staples.*

4 With brads, nail the rope molding onto the face of the door over the edges of the screen. Set nails. Fill holes with wood filler; let dry, then sand smooth. Touch up with *burnt sienna.*

5 Attach door with hinges, predrilling holes using the ⁵⁄₃₂-inch bit.

6 Glue ¾-inch piece of ⅛-inch dowel into the wooden knob. With the ⅛-inch drill bit, predrill a ½-inch-deep hole on the door for the knob, and glue opposite end of dowel into hole to attach knob.

7 Install magnetic catch, drilling pilot holes for screws.

8 Seal and protect cabinet with several coats of satin varnish. ●

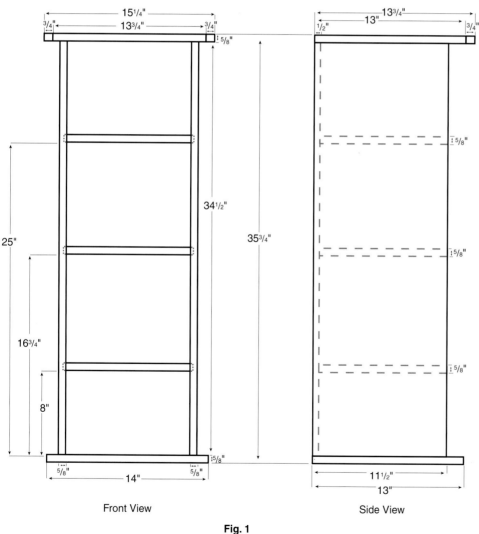

Front View   Side View

Fig. 1

SIMPLY CDs

Design by Angie Kopacek

Practice making rabbets and dadoes with this useful, quick-to-build cabinet.

CUTTING

1 Rip the ¾-inch oak plywood into two 6¼x30-inch pieces; from each piece, cut one 12¼-inch length (for top/bottom) and one 13-inch length (for side). **Note:** Use a stop block to make sure the lengths of both pieces are the same.

2 Rip the ½-inch oak plywood with the grain to 5¾ inches, then cut it to 12¼ inches (for shelf).

RABBETS & DADOES

1 Rout rabbets on the inside top and bottom edges of each side, ⅜-inch deep and ¹¹⁄₁₆-inch wide (Fig 1). **Note:** Use a router table and a straight bit, if possible, to ensure evenly cut rabbets. These rabbets are intentionally cut slightly short so the ends will be flush after banding.

2 On top, bottom and each side piece, rout a rabbet on the inside back edge ⅜-inch deep and ⁷⁄₁₆-inch wide (Fig 2).

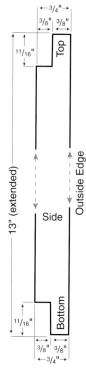

Fig. 1
Rout rabbets on inside top and bottom edges of each side.

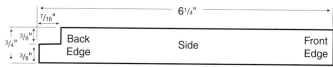

Fig. 2
Rout rabbets on inside back edges of top, bottom and both sides.

3 Set the router table fence 6¼ inches away from the router bit. With the top edge of one side piece next to the fence, use the ½-inch plywood router bit to cut a dado ⅜ inch deep and ½ inch wide. **Note:** *If ½-inch plywood bit is not available, make two passes with the ¼-inch bit).* Repeat for second side piece.

4 Dry-fit the top, bottom and shelf to the sides. Measure the opening for the back. Cut back to fit from ½-inch plywood (12⅜x12¼ inches on model project with grain running vertically). **Note:** *Take extra care when cutting the back as it will ensure the case is square.* Sand all pieces with 180-grit sandpaper.

ASSEMBLE & FINISH

Note: *Adhere blue masking tape along inside shoulder of all rabbets and dadoes to protect case from glue ooze and make clean-up easy.*

1 Glue shelf in side dadoes, then glue bottom and top in place. Make sure the case is square; clamp to secure. Add glue to the back rabbet and nail the back in place. Let dry completely. Remove masking tape.

2 Set the iron to the dry cotton setting. Beginning with the ⅜-inch-wide edges on the top and bottom of the case, apply oak veneer iron-on edge tape with the iron, then use scrap wood to press tape into plywood as

glue cools and sets. **Note:** *If a mistake is made, reheat to remove tape and start over.*

3 Use edge trimmer or chisel to trim away excess banding from the sides first, then the ends. **Note:** *When trimming the sides, find the direction where the grain of the banding is running away from the side and trim that direction to prevent being pulled into and gouging the side.* Scoring both sides of the banding will prevent tear-out. After trimming, lightly sand the corner and the veneer tape with 180-grit sandpaper.

4 In same manner, cover the front edges of the sides, running the tape all the way from the top to the bottom, then covering the front edges of the top, bottom and shelf. **Note:** *Cut banding slightly long, then butt one end tight against the side band; iron on and trim for a perfect fit. Band the back if desired.*

5 Using the foam brush, flood the surface with stain following manufacturer's instructions, staining the inside of the case first, then the outside and working with small areas at a time.

6 Apply topcoat with a clean rag and just enough sealer to barely wet the surface. Apply three coats, sanding lightly with steel wool after the first and second coat. Allow third coat to dry completely. ●

CHERRY KITCHEN BASE CABINET

Design by Anna Thompson

According to the designer, every girl should know how to build her own kitchen cabinets!

PROJECT NOTE

If building a series of cabinets to fill a wall space, calculate the width of the units in increments of 3 inches. If wall space does not measure evenly in 3-inch increments, adjust the width of the face frames or install purchased filler strips for an exact fit.

PROJECT SIZE
34¼x25x34¼ inches

TOOLS

- Table saw or circular saw
- Miter saw
- Router with ¼- and ¾-inch straight bits and ⁵⁄₁₆-inch rabbeting bit
- Router table
- Clamps
- Jigsaw
- Drill with ⅛- and ¼-inch straight bits, ⅜-inch countersink bit and #5 Vix bit
- Dowelling jig with ⁵⁄₁₆-inch bit

SUPPLIES

- ¾-inch birch plywood: 4x8 feet
- ¼-inch birch plywood: 4x4 feet
- ¼-inch cherry plywood: 4x4 feet
- ¾x1½-inch cherry*: two 8-foot lengths
- ¾x2-inch cherry*: two 6-foot lengths
- ⅝x4-inch oak*: two 6-foot lengths
- ⅝x5-inch cherry*: 3 feet
- 1½x25x34¼-inch maple butcher block
- Wood glue
- Coarse-thread dry-wall screws: 1-, 1¼-, 1⅝- and 2½-inch
- 24 (⁵⁄₁₆-inch) dowel pins
- ¾- and 1½-inch brads
- ⅜-inch flush plugs (optional)
- Two pair 2½-inch non-mortise hinges
- Two magnetic door catches with metal plates
- Four door/drawer pulls with screws**
- One pair 22-inch full-extension side-mount drawer slides
- Deft oil stain: medium walnut #305
- Sandpaper

* Mesurements given are actual, not nominal. Standard nominal lumber will need to be ripped and/or planed to size.

** Screws will need to be at least 1½ inches long to attach pulls to drawers.

Case
CUTTING

1 Referring to cutting chart for ¾-inch birch plywood, crosscut 32½ inches from one end and 31¼ inches from the opposite end. With the factory edge against the table-saw fence for each cut, rip the 32½-inch length into two 23¼-inch widths for sides (A); rip the 31¼-inch length into two 23-inch widths for top and bottom (B).

2 From the remainder of the ¾-inch plywood, crosscut one 12¼x30¼-inch piece for shelf (S) and rip a 3½x48-inch piece. Cut the 3½-inch-wide piece to 30½ inches long for the back cleat (C); rip the offcut into two 1¼-inch widths and cut into two 12-inch lengths for shelf cleats (R) and one 5½-inch length for doorstop (L).

3 From the ¼-inch birch plywood, cut a 31¼x31¼-inch piece for back (D). ***Note:*** *This will help keep the case square during assembly.*

Note: Refer to Fig. 1 for steps 4, 5 and 6.

4 Using the router with a ¾-inch straight bit and either a straightedge and clamps or an edge guide, cut identical ¾-inch-wide, ⅜-

inch-deep dados across the inside surface of each side (A) ½ inch from the top and 4¼ inches from the bottom.

5 Change to the ⁵⁄₁₆-inch rabbeting bit and cut a ⅜-inch-deep rabbet from top to bottom along the back inside edge of each side piece.

6 Clamp sides (A) together face to face with all edges flush. Measure and mark 4 inches from the bottom front corner and 3¼ inches in from the front. Square up this rectangle then cut out with the jigsaw to make the toe kick.

ASSEMBLY

Note: *Predrill for screws and countersink holes throughout.*

1 Dry-fit the top and bottom (B) into dadoes in sides (A) flush at the front. Disassemble and make adjustments if necessary.

2 Spread wood glue in dadoes; assemble top and bottom (B) to sides (A) flush at the front. Secure with four 1⅝-inch screws through sides (A) into ends of top and bottom (B).

3 Position back cleat (C) between sides and under top, flush with back rabbets and tops of sides; secure with 1⅝-inch countersunk screws driven through the sides into the ends of the cleat. Tack the back (D) in place to help keep the unit square. ***Note:*** *The back extends all the way down to the floor.*

4 Measure from outside edge to outside edge across bottom front; cut ¼-inch cherry plywood to this measurement (approximately 4x31¼ inches) for toe kick (E). Glue and tack in place.

Face frame
CUTTING

1 From the ¾x1½-inch cherry, cut two 28⅝-inch lengths for stiles (H) and three 29¼-inch lengths for top, bottom and middle rails (G).

2 Referring to Fig. 2, lay out the stiles, and top and bottom rails on the work surface. Set the third rail in place so there is a 5-inch opening for the top

drawer, then measure between the top of the bottom rail and the bottom of the center rail; cut ¾x1½-inch cherry to this measurement (19⅛ inches) for center stile (F).

ASSEMBLY

1 Position center stile (F) in the center of the middle and bottom rails (G); mark placement of center stile onto edges of middle and bottom rails. ***Note:*** *There should be 1⅜ inches on each side of the center stile.*

2 Dry-fit face frame together with dowel pins (Fig. 2): first dowelling the center stile to the middle and bottom rails, then dowelling the rails to the stiles one stile at a time. Glue together and clamp until set. Sand all joints smooth.

3 Attach face frame to case front with glue and small nails. ***Option:*** *Attach frame to case with 1⅝-inch predrilled, countersunk screws: then plug with cherry plugs.*

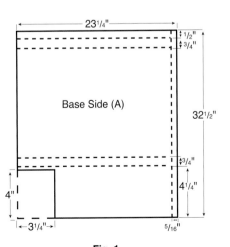

Fig. 1
Cut dadoes and rabbets.

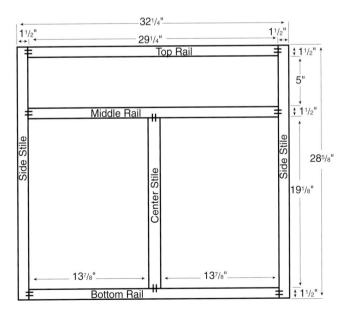

Fig. 2
Base Face Frame

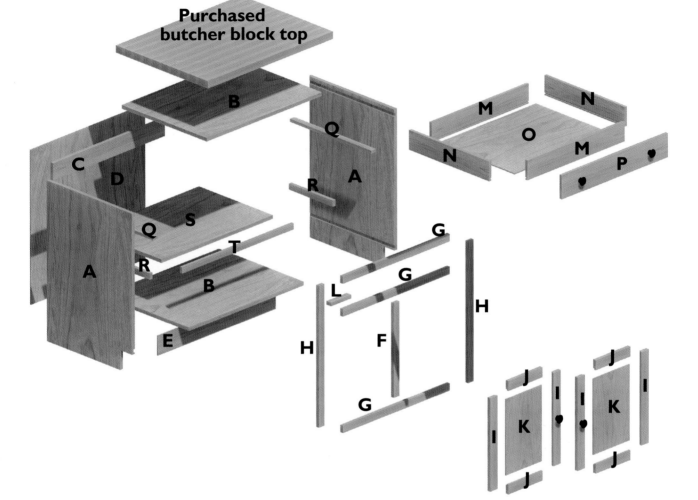

Purchased butcher block top

CHERRY KITCHEN BASE CABINET CUTTING CHART (Actual Sizes)				
P	T	W	L	#
A	¾"	23¼"	32½"	2
B	¾"	23"	31¼"	2
C	¾"	3½"	30½"	1
D	¼"	31¼"	31¼"	1
E	¼"	4"	32"	1
F	¾"	1½"	19⅛"	1
G	¾"	1½"	29¼"	3

H	¾"	1½"	28⅝"	2
I	¾"	2"	18⅞"	4
J	¾"	2"	9⅝"	4
K	¼"	10⅛"	15⅜"	2
L	¾"	1¼"	5½"	1
M	⅝"	4"	26¾"	2
N	⅝"	4"	22"	2
O	¼"	21⅛"	27⅛"	1

P	⅝"	4⅞"	29⅛"	1
Q	⅝"	1¼"	22⅛"	2
R	¾"	1¼"	12"	2
S	¾"	12¼"	30¼"	1
T	⅝"	1¼"	30¼"	1

Doors
CUTTING

1 From the ¾x2-inch cherry, cut four 18⅞-inch lengths for door stiles (I) and four 9⅝-inch lengths for door rails (J).

2 Referring to Fig. 3, lay out the door frames with the door rails (J) butting into the door stiles (I) flush at the top and bottom of the frame. Mark dowel locations and drill holes for two ⁵⁄₁₆-inch dowel pins in each joint.

3 Dry-fit the door frames together; measure the inside edge from side to side and top to bottom for door panel size. From ¼-inch cherry plywood, cut two door panels (K) ½ inch bigger than each of the panel measurements (approximately 10⅛x15⅜ inches). Set door panels aside.

ASSEMBLY

Note: Predrill for screws and countersink holes throughout.

1 Mark the inside edge of each door rail and stile, then disassemble door frame. Use the router table and the ¼-

inch straight bit to cut a ⁵⁄₁₆-inch deep dado on the inside edges of the door frames. Center dado on the thickness of each rail and stile, cutting the full length of the rail and beginning and ending 1⅝ inches from each end of the stile. Make two passes to get the full ⁵⁄₁₆-inch depth.

2 Glue one door stile into the rails, then slide the panel in place and glue the remaining stile in place. ***Note:*** *Do not glue the panels.* Let dry; sand all joints flush. Using Vix bit and screws provided with hinges, install doors into frame openings with 2½-inch non-mortise hinges.

3 On the inside of the case, center doorstop (L) over the center stile and flush at the bottom with the top of the center rail. Fasten with glue and 1⅝-inch screws.

4 Install magnetic door catches to the doorstop and the metal plates to the corresponding corners of the doors. Attach pulls centered in each door stile and 1 inch from the top of each door rail.

Drawer
CUTTING

1 From the inside, measure the space between the side of the case and

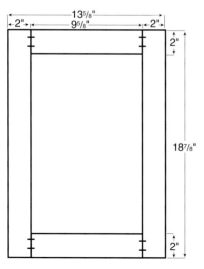

Fig. 3
Base Door Frame

the edge of the face frame at the drawer opening. From one 6-foot ⅝x4-inch oak board, cut a 22⅛-inch length; rip this length into two 1¼-inch widths for drawer slide supports (Q). **Note:** *If the space between the side and the edge of the face frame is ¾ inch, cut supports from a leftover piece of the ¾-inch birch plywood instead of the ⅝-inch oak.*

2 On each of the remaining ⅝x4-inch oak boards, cut a ¼-inch-wide, ¼-inch-deep dado ¼ inch from one long edge. Cut two 22-inch lengths for drawer sides (N) and two 26¾-inch lengths for drawer box front and back (M). **Note:** *The dadoed edge is the bottom inside edge of each piece.*

3 From ¼-inch cherry plywood, cut a piece 21⅛x27⅛ inches for drawer bottom (O).

4 Measure the drawer opening in the case; cut and rip the ⅝x5-inch cherry ⅛ inch less in height and width than this measurement (4⅞x29⅛ inches on model project) for drawer face (P).

ASSEMBLY

1 Assemble the drawer box by butting the drawer box front (M) into the sides (N) and driving 1¼-inch screws through the sides into the ends of the front. Slide the bottom (O) in place, then attach the back (M) in the same manner as the front.

2 Center the drawer face (P) on the drawer box front side to side. Attach by driving a 1-inch screw at each corner through the inside of the drawer box front and into the back of the drawer face. Countersink just enough for the screw heads to be flush with the inside of the drawer box.

3 Position drawer slide supports (Q) to insides of case sides so drawer slides will be centered on the supports when installed; attach with three screws driven through each support into the case side. Install drawer slides following manufacturer's instructions.

4 Mark desired placement of drawer pulls on drawer face; attach with screws, predrilling through drawer face and box front.

FINAL ASSEMBLY & FINISHING

1 Using glue and countersunk 1¼-inch screws, attach the two shelf cleats (R) inside case so tops are 9¼ inches from the case bottom.

2 Rip and cut a leftover piece of ⅝x4-inch oak to 1¼x30¼ inches for shelf trim (T). Using glue and 1½-inch brads, attach trim to front of shelf (S). Let dry.

3 Finish-sand case, drawer, doors and shelf; apply oil stain following manufacturer's instructions.

4 Set the shelf on cleats. Place the maple butcher block on top of the case, centered side to side and flush with the back. Attach it to the case by driving 2½-inch screws through the case top (B) and into the bottom of the butcher-block top. ●

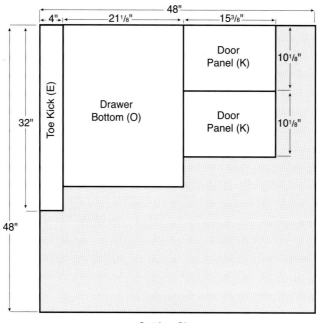

Cutting Chart
¼" Cherry Plywood

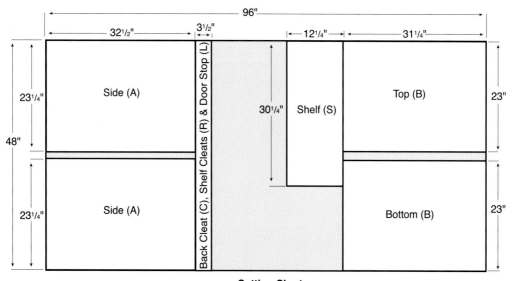

Cutting Chart
¾" Birch Plywood

CHERRY KITCHEN UPPER CABINET

Design by Anna Thompson

Glass-front doors let you display grandma's heirloom china in style.

PROJECT NOTE

If building a series of cabinets to fill a wall space, calculate the width of the units in increments of 3 inches. If wall space does not measure evenly in 3-inch increments, adjust the width of the face frames or install purchased filler strips for an exact fit.

PROJECT SIZE
31¼x12⅝x30 inches

TOOLS
- Table saw
- Miter saw
- Router with ⅜-inch rabbeting bit, ¾-inch straight bit, 5⁄16-inch rabbetting bit and router table
- Drill with ⅛- and ¼-inch straight bits, ⅜-inch countersink bit, and #5 Vix bit
- Dowel jig with 5⁄16-inch bit
- Chisel
- Clamps

SUPPLIES
- ¾-inch cherry plywood: one 4x4-foot sheet
- ¼-inch cherry plywood: one 4x4-foot sheet
- ¼x¾-inch screen molding: 3 feet
- ¾x¾-inch hardwood: 3 feet
- ¾x1½-inch cherry*: two 6-foot lengths
- ¾x2-inch cherry*: two 8-foot lengths
- Sandpaper
- 10x20-inch piece of ¼-inch pegboard
- 32 (5⁄16-inch) dowel pins
- 1⅝- and 2-inch coarse-thread drywall screws
- Wood glue
- ⅜-inch cherry (or birch) flush plugs (optional)
- Two pair 2½-inch non-mortise hinges
- Deft oil stain: medium walnut #305
- Two 10x23½-inch pieces single-strength glass
- Two door pulls with screws
- Glazier's points and clear caulk
- Four ¼-inch adjustable shelf pegs

* Measurements given are actual, not nominal. Standard nominal lumber will need to be ripped and/or planed to size.

Case
CUTTING

1 Referring to cutting chart for ¾-inch cherry plywood, crosscut 31⅛ inches from one end and 10 inches from the opposite end. Rip the 31⅛-inch length into four 11⅞-inch-wide boards: two for sides (A) and two for top and bottom (B). Cut each of the sides (A) to 30 inches long; rip the 10-inch board to 30¼ inches for the shelf (K).

2 From screen molding, cut a 30¼-inch length for shelf back (L). From ¾x¾-inch hardwood cut a 30¼-inch length for shelf front (M).

3 From ¼-inch cherry plywood, cut a 30x31⅛-inch piece for back (D). *Note: This will help keep the case square during assembly.*

4 Using the router with a ¾-inch straight bit and either a straight-edge and clamps, an edge guide or a dado jig refer to Fig. 1 to cut identical ¾-inch-wide, 5⁄16-inch-deep dados across the inside surface of each side (A) ½ inch from the top and from the bottom edges.

5 Change to the ⁵⁄₁₆-inch rabbeting bit and cut a ⅜-inch-deep rabbet along the inside back edges of both sides (A).

6 On the inside of each side (A), draw a light line across the width of each side 8½ inches from the bottom and 10 inches from the top for shelf placement; measure in from the front edge and the inside of the back rabbet 1 inch and draw a light line between the two horizontal lines in the front and back. Set a stop or mark the ¼-inch drill bit with tape; drill ⅜ inch deep. Using a 10- to 12-inch piece of ¼-inch peg board as a template to evenly space holes, drill along each reference line for adjustable shelf pegs.

ASSEMBLY

Note: Predrill for screws and countersink holes throughout.

1 Dry-fit the top and bottom (B) into the dadoes in the sides (A) flush at the front; disassemble and make adjustments if necessary. Spread wood glue in dadoes and assemble top, bottom and sides, securing with two or three 1⅝-inch coarse-thread drywall screws driven through sides into the ends of the top and bottom.

2 Measure across the top back on the inside of the case. From the leftover ¾-inch cherry plywood, rip and crosscut a ¾x2-inch piece to that measurement (30½ inches) for the hanging cleat (C). Position cleat between sides (A) flush with rabbet and tops of sides; secure with 1⅝-inch screws driven through sides into the ends of the cleat. *Note: Be careful not to countersink too deeply as there is already a ⁵⁄₁₆-inch deep dado on the opposite side.*

3 Glue and tack the screen molding (L) to the back of the shelf (K). Glue and tack the ¾-inch hardwood (M) to the front of the shelf. Let dry.

Face frame
CUTTING

1 From the ¾x1½-inch cherry, cut two 30-inch lengths for side stiles (E) and two 29¼-inch lengths for rails (F).

2 Referring to Fig. 2, lay out the stiles and rails on the work surface. Measure the distance between the bottom of the top rail and the top of the bottom rail; cut a length of ¾x2-inch cherry to this measurement (27 inches) for center stile (G); center between side stiles.

ASSEMBLE

1 Mark dowel locations at the corner joints and centers of rails. Drill dowel holes, then dry-fit face frame together. Disassemble and adjust as needed, then glue together and clamp until set. Sand all joints smooth.

2 With glue and small nails, attach face frame to case front flush at the top and evenly spaced at the sides. *Option: Attach frame to case with 1⅝-inch predrilled, countersunk screws, then plug with flush plugs.*

Door frames
CUTTING

1 From ¾x2-inch cherry, cut four 26⅞-inch lengths for door stiles (H) and four 9½-inch lengths for door rails (I).

2 From the remaining ¾x1½-inch cherry, cut one 6½-inch length for doorstop (J).

3 Referring to Fig. 3, lay out the door frames with the door rails (I) butted into the door stiles (H) flush at the top and bottom of the frame. Mark dowel locations and drill holes for two ⁵⁄₁₆-inch dowel pins in each joint.

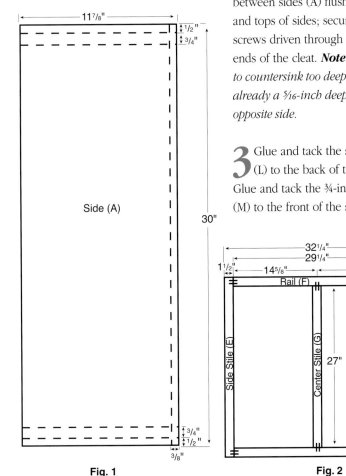

Fig. 1
Side Dadoes & Rabbet

Fig. 2
Upper Cabinet Face Frame

P	T	W	L	#
A	¾"	11⅞"	30"	2
B	¾"	11⅞"	31⅛"	2
C	¾"	2"	30½"	1
D	¼"	30"	31⅛"	1
E	¾"	1½"	30"	2
F	¾"	1½"	29¼"	2
G	¾"	2"	27"	1
H	¾"	2"	26⅞"	4
I	¾"	2"	9½"	4
J	¾"	1½"	6½"	1
K	¾"	10"	30¼"	1
L	¼"	¾"	30¼"	1
M	¾"	¾"	30¼"	1

CHERRY KITCHEN
UPPER CABINET
CUTTING CHART
(Actual Sizes)

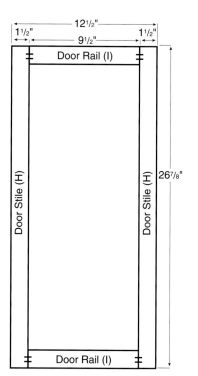

Fig. 3
Upper Cabinet Door Frame

ASSEMBLY DIAGRAM

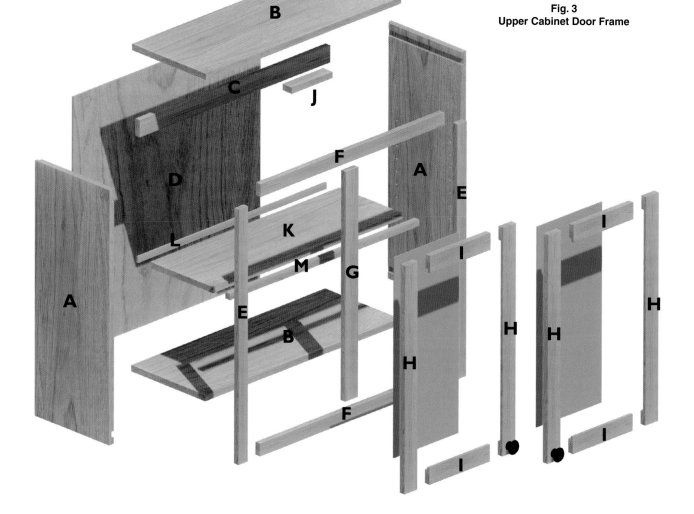

ASSEMBLY

Note: Predrill for screws and countersink holes throughout.

1 Dry-fit door frames together; adjust fit if needed. Glue up door frames. Using the router and the ⅜-inch rabbeting bit, cut a ⅜x⅜-inch rabbet on the inside back edge of the door frames for glass panels. Gently square up the corners of the rabbet with a sharp chisel.

2 Position doorstop (J) to the back of the face frame, centered over the center stile and flush with the bottom of the top rail. Attach with 2-inch screws countersunk just enough to make the screw heads flush.

FINAL ASSEMBLY & FINISHING

1 Using Vix bit and screws provided with hinges, install doors into frame openings with 2½-inch non-mortise hinges. Install magnetic door catches to door stop (J) and the corresponding metal plates to door corners.

2 Predrill holes for door pulls centered on the door stile and 1 inch from the bottom of the door; attach pulls with accompanying screws.

3 Remove hardware. Finish-sand the case, shelf and door frames and apply oil stain following manufacturer's instructions.

4 Install glass panels in door frames; secure with glazier's points and clear caulk.

5 Put shelf pegs in holes and set shelf in place. Replace hardware. ●

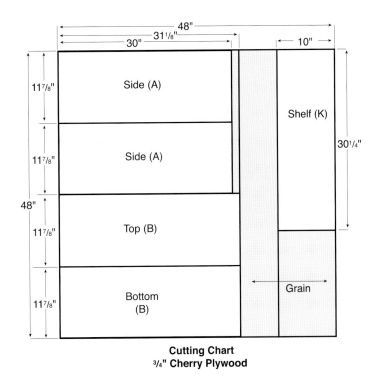

Cutting Chart
¾" Cherry Plywood

OFFICE IN AN ARMOIRE

Design by Anna Thompson

Hide your home office—the computer and cables and stacks of papers—in a stylish armoire, complete with swing-out storage.

PROJECT NOTE

Predrill for screws and countersink holes throughout.

Case

CUTTING

1 Referring to cutting chart for ¾-inch birch plywood (sheet No. 1), set the table-saw fence 7¾ inches from the blade and rip full 96-inch length. Crosscut this strip into two 39½-inch lengths for case top cleat and desk cleat (C).

2 From the remainder of sheet No. 1, crosscut at 64 inches, then rip into two 20-inch widths for case sides (A); cut and rip a 19¾x40-inch piece for desktop (B) and a 9¼x39½-inch piece for base cleat (D).

3 Referring to cutting chart for ¾-inch birch plywood (sheet No. 2), crosscut at 20¾ inches from one end, then rip that piece to 41 inches long for case top (L). Crosscut another piece 18 inches wide and rip it to 39¼ inches long for adjustable shelf (I). Set the remainder of sheet No. 2 aside for pullout.

4 Measure 31¼ inches from the bottom of each case side (A) and mark for bottom edge of dado. With inside surfaces up, clamp case sides (A) together on work surface, side by side with edges flush. With the ¾-inch straight bit in the router, use the dado jig, or clamps and a straightedge as router guides to cut a ¼-inch-deep dado across both sides at this mark.

5 Change to the 5⁄16-inch rabbetting bit and rout a ¼-inch-deep rabbet the full length of each side along the back inside edge.

PROJECT SIZE

44x22¼x64¾ inches

TOOLS

- Table saw or circular saw
- Miter saw
- Clamps
- Router with ¾-inch straight, ⅜-inch and 5⁄16-inch rabbetting and ⅜-inch roundover bits
- Drill with ⅛-inch straight, ⅜-inch countersink and #5 Vix bits

SUPPLIES

- ¾-inch birch plywood: two 4x8-foot sheets
- ¼-inch lauan or birch plywood: one 4x8-foot sheet
- 1x1 poplar: one 4-foot length
- 1x2 poplar: one 10-foot, two 8-foot and one 4-foot lengths
- 1x4 poplar: one 5-foot length
- 1⅛-inch cove mold trim: one 8-foot length
- ½-inch lauan or birch plywood: one 4x8-foot sheet
- ¼-inch birch plywood: one 4x4-foot sheet
- ¼x¾-inch screen molding: three 6-foot lengths
- Coarse-thread dry-wall screws: ¾-, 1¼-, 1⅝- and 2-inch
- ¾-inch brads
- Wood glue
- Three door pulls
- Four 2½-inch heavy-duty casters with #10x¾-inch screws
- ⅜-inch flush birch plugs
- Desired finish
- Three pairs 2x⅜-inch inset hinges
- One pair magnetic door catches with metal plates

6 From the 4x8 sheet of ¼-inch lauan or birch plywood, cut a 40x64-inch piece for case back (E).

7 Cut the 1x1 poplar to 37¾ inches long for shelf back trim (J); cut 1x2 poplar to 37¾ inches long for shelf front trim (K) and 39½ inches for frame trim support (F).

8 From the 1x4 poplar, cut two 8½-inch lengths; rip each length into two ⅞-inch widths for 2 each front and back shelf standards (G). Clamp all four shelf standards together with the ¾-inch width down, then rout ¾-inch dadoes across all four boards ¾ inch apart (Fig. 1).

9 From the remaining 43-inch length of 1x4 poplar, rip a ¾-inch width; cut two 19-inch lengths from this width for shelf supports (H). Set the 2⅝-inch width aside for use in a later step.

ASSEMBLY

Note: *If preferred, cleats and desktop may be secured with 1½-inch finish nails instead of screws.*

1 Slip desktop (B) into the dados in the case sides (A) flush with front edges; secure with glue and 1⅝-inch screws driven through the sides into the ends of the desk top.

2 Position each cleat as follows between case sides and flush with rabbetted edge, then secure by driving 1⅝-inch screws through sides into ends of cleats: case top cleat (C) flush with top edges; desk cleat (C) butted into bottom of desktop; and base cleat (D) flush with bottom edges.

3 Attach case back (E) with ¾-inch screws driven into the rabbet and also into the three cleats (C and D) and the back of the desktop (B).

4 Secure the face trim support (F) so the 1½-inch width is flush with the top of the sides, and the ¾-inch thickness is flush with the front of the sides.

5 With the dentil cuts facing the front of the case, butt the two back shelf standards (G) into the bottom of the top cleat (C) and against the case back; secure with glue and 1¼-inch screws driven through the standards into the sides.

P	T	W	L	#
A	¾"	20"	64"	2
B	¾"	19¾"	40"	1
C	¾"	7¾"	39½"	2
D	¾"	9¼"	39½"	1
E	¼"	40"	64"	1
F	¾"	1½"	39½"	1
G	¾"	⅞"	8½"	4
H	¾"	¾"	19"	2
I	¾"	18"	39¼"	1
J	¾"	¾"	37¾"	1
K	¾"	1½"	37¾"	1
L	¾"	20¾"	41"	1
M	¾"	1½"	64"	2
N	¾"	1½"	38"	1
O	¾"	2⅝"	38"	1
P	¾"	1½"	5½"	1
Q	¾"	1½"	44"	1
R	¾"	1½"	22¼"	2
S	¾"	1⅛"	42½"	1
T	¾"	1⅛"	21½"	2
U	½"	19¼"	30"	2
V	¼"	2¼"	30"	4
W	¼"	2¼"	14¾"	4
X	¾"	17⅞"	25"	3
Y	¾"	17⅞"	30"	2
Z	¼"	¾"	17⅞"	3
AA	¼"	¾"	30½"	1
AB	¼"	¾"	30¼"	1

OFFICE IN AN ARMOIRE CUTTING CHART (Actual Sizes)

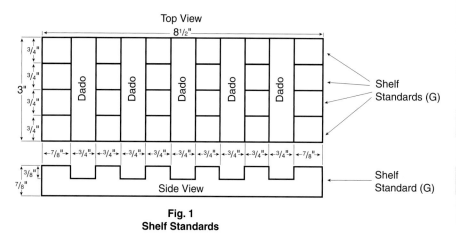

Fig. 1
Shelf Standards

ASSEMBLY DIAGRAM

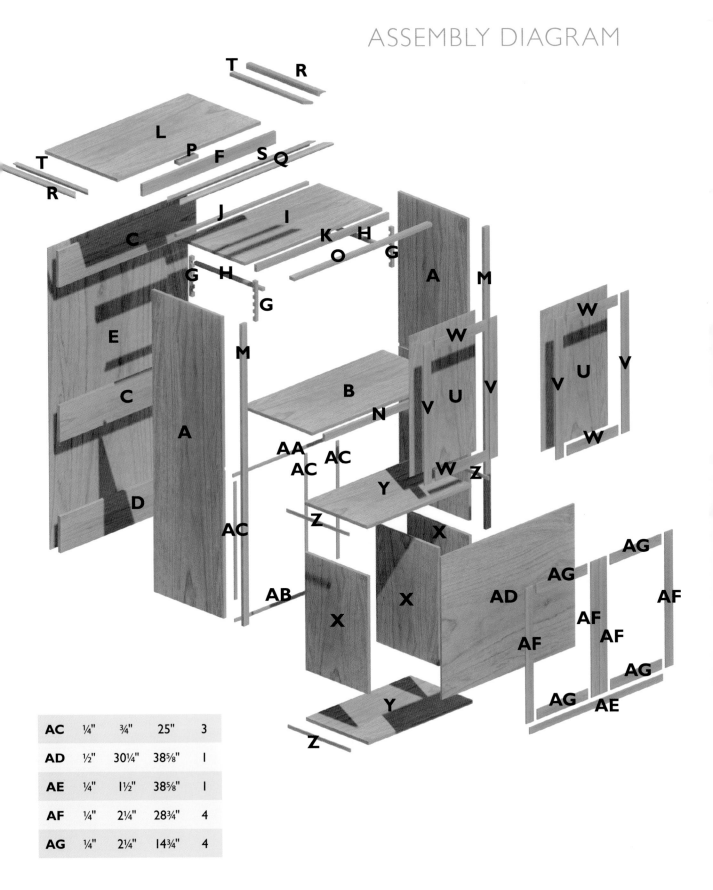

AC	¼"	¾"	25"	3
AD	½"	30¼"	38⅝"	1
AE	¼"	1½"	38⅝"	1
AF	¼"	2¼"	28¾"	4
AG	¼"	2¼"	14¾"	4

6 From the front edge of the back standards measure and mark each side 18⅛ inches toward the front and 7¾ inches from the top. Position front shelf standards with the top of the standard at the 7¾-inch marks and the dentil side against the 18⅛-inch mark; secure in same manner as for back shelf standards (Fig. 2).

7 Center the ¾x¾x37¾-inch shelf back trim (J) on the back edge of the shelf (I) and secure with glue and 1½-inch nails. Repeat to attach the ¾x 1½x37¾-inch shelf front trim (K) flush at the top (Fig. 3).

8 With glue and 1⅝-inch screws, attach case top (L) to the case sides (A) and top cleat (C), flush with case back (E) and sides, driving screws through the top and into the ends of the sides. Also drive several 1¼-inch screws up through the face trim cleat into the bottom of the top.

Case face frame & trim
CUTTING

1 From 10-foot 1x2, cut one 64-inch length for face frame stile (M); set remaining length aside. From one 8-foot 1x2, cut one 64-inch length for second face frame stile (M) and one 5½-inch length for door-catch support (P). Using glue and 1⅝-inch screws, attach face frame stiles (M) to fronts of case sides (A) and into the face trim support (F) with outside, top and bottom edges flush to the side (A).

2 Measure the distance between the stiles at desktop (B). From the remaining 10-foot 1x2 poplar, cut a piece to this length (38 inches) for desktop face (N). Position between face frame stiles (M) so top of face is flush with the top of the desktop (B); attach by driving 1⅝-inch screws through the desktop face (N) into the edge of the desktop (B).

3 Measure the distance between the stiles at the case top. From the 2⅝-inch width set aside in step 8 of case cutting instructions, cut a piece to this length (38 inches) for the top face rail (O). Position between face frame stiles (M) and butted into the bottom of case top (L), flush at front; secure with 1⅝-inch screws through the face (O) and into the face trim support (F). These screws will be covered by the top trim.

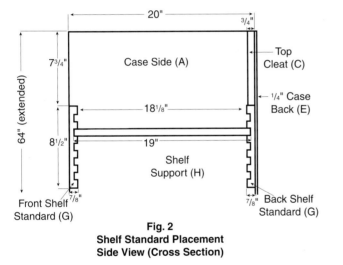

Fig. 2
Shelf Standard Placement
Side View (Cross Section)

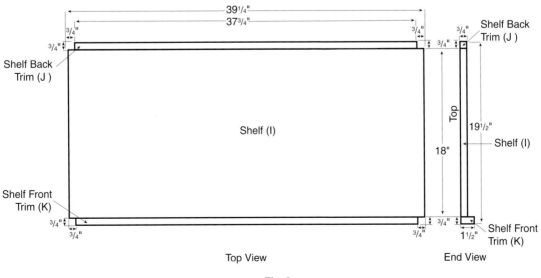

Top View

End View

Fig. 3
Shelf Assembly

4 Using the ⅜-inch roundover bit, rout a bull nose on both sides of one edge of the second 8-foot 1x2 poplar. From bull-nosed poplar, cut a piece mitered at both ends and measuring 44 inches from long point to long point (41 inches short point to short point) for front top trim (Q). Cut two pieces each mitered at one end only and measuring 22¼ inches from long point front to square back for side top trim (R).

5 From 1⅛-inch cove mold trim, cut a piece mitered at both ends and measuring 42½ inches long point to long point (41 inches short point to short point) for face trim (S); cut two mirrored pieces each mitered at one end only and measuring 21½ inches long point front to square back for side trim (T).

ASSEMBLY

1 Position one ¾-inch edge of the door-catch support (P) against the back of the top face rail (O) centered between the stiles; attach with 2-inch screws driven through the door-catch support into the back of the top face rail.

2 Attach front top trim (Q) and side top trim (R) to case top with glue and 2-inch countersunk screws or 2½-inch finish nails driven through the trim pieces into the ends of the case top.

3 Using glue and 1-inch nails, attach cove mold face trim (S) and side trim (T) around top of case butted into top and side trim (Q and R).

4 Plug screw holes with ⅜-inch plugs; sand flush.

Doors
CUTTING

1 Measure the door opening. Add ⅝ inch to each direction to accommodate clearance and door overlay; cut the ½-inch lauan or birch plywood to these measurements for door blank (38⅝x30 inches on model project). Rout a ⅜x⅜-inch rabbet around the perimeter of the door blank (Fig. 4). **Note:** *Handle with extreme care. The overlay on these doors is only ⅛ inch until the overlay pieces can be glued on in a few more steps.*

2 Find the center of the 38⅝-inch width and cut the door blank exactly in half creating two doors (U). Lay doors face up on work surface. **Note:** *Rabbet is on the inside, facing down.*

3 Set the table-saw fence 1½ inches from the blade; rip the entire length of the 4x4 foot ¼-inch birch plywood; set aside. Reset the fence to 2¼ inches and rip eight more 4-foot lengths for overlays. Set aside remainder for pullout door.

ASSEMBLY

1 From 2¼-inch overlay pieces, cut four 30-inch stiles (V). Glue and clamp to the face of each door flush at top and bottom, outside and center edges.

2 Measure the distance between stiles (14¾ inches) and cut four rails (W) from 2¼-inch overlay pieces. Glue and clamp the rails flush at the top and bottom of the doors between the stiles. Set remaining 2¼-inch overlay stock aside for pullout door panel overlays.

3 Predrill and install door pulls 15 inches from the top and 1⅛ inches from the center edge of each door.

Pullout case
CUTTING

1 Referring to cutting chart for ¾-inch birch veneer plywood (sheet No.

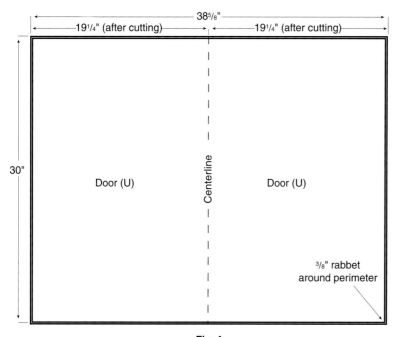

Fig. 4
Cut rabbeted door blank in half
to make two upper doors (U).

2) set the table-saw fence 17⅞ inches from the blade. From the remainder of ¾-inch birch veneer plywood (step 3 of case cutting instructions) rip one length, then cut the 30-inch width three times.

2 From the long 17⅞-inch piece, cut two 25-inch lengths for uprights (X). Cut one of the 17⅞x30-inch pieces to 25 inches long for the third upright (X). Set the two remaining 17⅞x30-inch pieces aside for top and bottom (Y).

3 From the screen molding cut three 17⅞-inch lengths for side trim (Z), one 30½-inch length for top front trim (AA), one 30¼-inch length for bottom front trim (AB), and three 25-inch lengths for upright trim (AC).

ASSEMBLY

1 Butt two uprights (X) into top and bottom (Y) flush with ends. Secure with glue and 1⅝-inch screws. Slide the remaining upright (X) into place so there are 8¼ inches between it and the left upright.

2 Glue and use brads to nail the side trim (Z) to edges of both top and bottom on the right side of pullout, and to edge of top only on the left side.

3 Glue and nail the top front trim (AA) to the front edge of the top, and the bottom front trim (AB) to the front edge of the bottom.

4 Glue and nail the upright trim pieces (AC) to front edges of uprights. **Note:** *Trim length if necessary.*

5 Turn pullout upside down and install 2½-inch casters at corners.

Pullout door panel
CUTTING

1 From the ½-inch Lauan or birch plywood, cut a piece 30¼x38⅝ inches for pullout door panel (AD).

2 From the 1½-inch-wide overlay pieces set aside in step 3 of cutting instructions for doors, cut a 38⅝-inch length for door panel bottom rail (AE); clamp rail to bottom of pullout door panel with bottom and side edges flush.

3 From the remaining 2¼-inch-wide overlay stock, cut four 28¾-inch pieces for door panel stiles (AF). Referring to Figure 5, clamp two of the stiles to the pullout door panel with outside and top edges flush. Clamp the remaining two stiles to the center of the pullout door panel, flush at the top, and with a ⅛-inch gap between stiles to create the effect of a double door. **Note:** *There should be a slight gap between the bottoms of the stiles and the top of the bottom rail.*

4 From the 2¼-inch-wide overlay stock, cut four 14¾-inch pieces for door panel rails (AG). Check fit between the stiles; adjust if necessary, then remove clamps and overlays.

5 On the front of the door panel, draw a horizontal line across the panel 2¼ inches from the top and 3¾ inches from the bottom for reference in attaching the pullout.

6 On the opposite (back) side of the panel, rout a ⅜x⅜-inch rabbet around the perimeter. **Note:** *Handle carefully to prevent break out of the 1/8 inch lip.* Draw horizontal lines 2¼ and 28¾ inches from the bottom of the panel. Measuring from the left side of the panel and the inside edge of the rabbet, draw vertical lines 1½ and 31½ inches.

7 Drill ⅛-inch pilot holes evenly spaced just inside the perimeter of this outline. Set pullout face down and

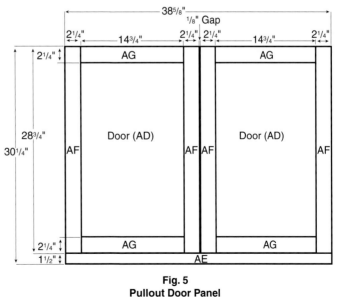

Fig. 5
Pullout Door Panel
Overlay Layout

place the back of the door panel on top of it so the pullout is inside the outline. Secure pullout to door panel with 1⅝-inch screws, countersunk just until heads are flush.

8 Glue and clamp the door-panel overlays on the front of the door panel in the same order in which they were cut: bottom rail (AE), stiles (AF) and door-panel rails (AG), maintaining the ⅛-inch gap between the two center stiles.

9 Install the door pull 1⅜ inches from the top and 1⅜ inches from the left side of the pullout.

FINISHING

1 Remove door pulls. Plug exposed screw holes and sand flush. Finish sand surfaces.

2 Paint or stain as desired following manufacturer's instructions.

3 Reinstall door pulls. Install hinges to right side of pullout and case. Install door catches to door-catch support and corresponding positions on insides of doors. ●

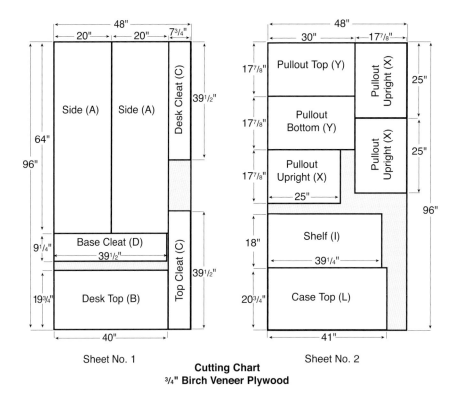

Sheet No. 1   Sheet No. 2

Cutting Chart
¾" Birch Veneer Plywood

BEDSIDE BOOKCASE

Design by Amy Phillips

A shelf holds essential bedtime reading, while a secret cubby holds tissues, cough drops and other necessities.

CUTTING

1 Rip the 4x5-foot sheet of ½-inch birch plywood into three 8-inch widths with the grain running along the 60-inch length. From the remaining 2-foot plywood, rip a 9½-inch width from one end for the front. **Note:** *Measure the height of the mattress and cut the front to that height minus the ½-inch thickness of the lid.* Set the rest of this plywood aside for back.

2 From the three 8-inch widths, cut two 29¾-inch lengths for the sides, one 23½-inch length for the top, one 22⅞-inch length for the lid and one 23¾-inch length for the shelf. Cut the 9½-inch front to 23 inches long.

3 Rip the 8x22⅞-inch lid and the 28x23¾-inch shelf each to 7½ inches wide.

4 Mark the lid 2¾ inches from the center front edge. With the 1-inch spade bit, drill a hole centered at this point. **Note:** *Drill half-way through the lid, then turn the lid over and finish drill-*

ing. Rout the top and bottom edges of the hole using the ⅜-inch roundover bit.

5 With the ½-inch straight bit, rout a ¼x¼-inch rabbet across the inside top of each side and across each end of the top on the inside for half laps (Fig. 1).

6 Mark the sides as right and left, and mark the front of the top. Rout a ¼x½-inch rabbet across the back inside edge of each side and the top to receive the back (Fig. 2)

7 From the remainder of the 4x5-foot sheet of birch plywood, cut a 23½x29½-inch piece for the back, with the grain running with the 29½ inches.

8 On the inside of each side, beginning

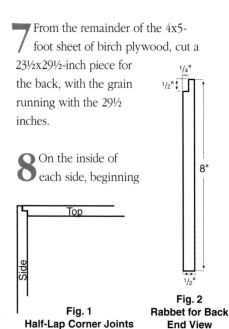

Fig. 1
Half-Lap Corner Joints

Fig. 2
Rabbet for Back
End View

PROJECT SIZE
24x32x24½-inches

TOOLS
- Table saw
- Router with ½-inch straight and ⅜-inch roundover bits
- Router table (optional)
- Drill with screw driver, ⅛- and ¼-inch bullet and 1-inch spade bits
- Clamps
- Pneumatic nailer with 1-inch brad nails

SUPPLIES
- ½-inch birch plywood: 4x5 feet

- ½-inch (or thicker) plywood: 24x36 inches (for base)
- ¼-inch pegboard: 8x12 inches
- Wood glue
- Two 1½-inch brass hinges
- ½-inch birch veneer iron-on edge tape: 12 feet
- 220-grit sandpaper
- Minwax Fruitwood stain
- Minwax Semi-gloss polyurethane
- Minwax colonial oak wood putty
- Two 1½-inch T-hinges
- Two 1½-inch hook-and-eye sets
- Four adjustable shelf pins

4½ inches from the top and 12 inches from the bottom, drill holes for adjustable shelf pins 1 inch from each edge. *Note: Cut a piece of pegboard and clamp in place to use as a guide, flipping it over when drilling holes on the second side. Use a wood spacer or mark depth with masking tape to be sure to not drill too deep.*

ASSEMBLE

1 Glue and nail through the sides into the top. Glue and nail the front piece in place, flush with the bottom and the face edges of the sides.

2 Determine which side of the back will face the front. Measure 10 inches from the bottom of the back (the width of the front piece plus ½ inch) and mark a reference line across the back for the hinges.

3 Place the box assembly over the back as it will be when assembled (nestle the back into the rabbets). Measure 4 inches from each side along the back reference line and place a hash-mark for hinge locations. Making sure the bottoms are flush, set the lid evenly spaced between the sides and transfer the hash mark to the top of the lid.

4 Measure the depth needed for the 1½-inch brass hinges and cut a notch into the lid at each hinge location. Install the 1½ inch brass

hinges. ***Note:*** *Double-check the screw length when attaching hinges. If greater that ½ inch, snip off the end with a wire cutter to make sure it does not protrude.* Check alignment and function of lid, then remove.

FINISH

1 Apply iron-on edge tape to all exposed plywood edges (faces of the sides, top, lid and shelf; the top of the front; and the ¼-inch exposed tops of the sides.) Trim edging tape flush.

2 Fill all nail holes and let dry. Sand all surfaces to prepare for staining. ***Note:*** *Be careful not to sand through the plywood veneer or the banding.*

3 Following manufacturer's instructions, apply stain to assembled box unit, shelf, lid, back and 24x36-inch base plywood; let dry. Apply one coat of polyurethane to all pieces following manufacturer's instructions. Let dry.

4 Sand lightly with 220-grit sandpaper; remove dust. Set the back in place and secure to the box with glue and 1-inch nails; remove excess glue.

5 Apply a second coat of polyure-thane to all pieces; let dry. Scuff surfaces with 220-grit sandpaper and apply a third coat of polyurethane; let dry.

6 Place 24x36-inch base flat on work surface; position box unit on base with back of unit flush with end of base. Referring to Fig. 3, attach back to base with T hinges.

7 Install hooks to the back of the box front, and the eyes to the base to hold box unit upright.

8 Reinstall hinges to lid, then attach lid to back. Lift mattress and slide base under it. Install shelf pins and set shelf in place. ●

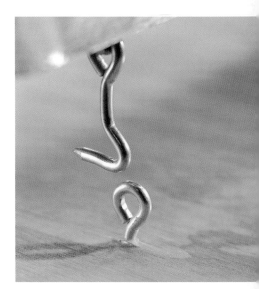

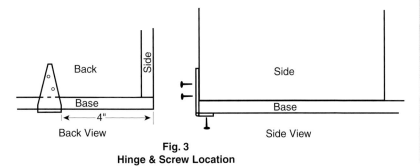

Fig. 3
Hinge & Screw Location

EASY ROOM DIVIDER

Design by Amy Phillips

Whether you need to divide a space or hide some clutter, this project makes it easy!

PROJECT OPTIONS
• Substitute pegboard or dry-erase board for the lauan.
• Adhere corkboard to center panels.
• Add a third or fourth section to divide a larger area.

CUTTING

1 Crosscut the lauan at 65 inches, then rip it in half lengthwise.

2 Cut each 2x2 pine board into one 72-inch stile and one 23½-inch rail. Examine each piece and mark the inside, top and bottom. ***Note:*** *The inside of the stiles and rails will house the lauan panel.*

3 On the end of one of the rails, mark the center. Set the table-saw blade to a height of ¼ inch, then set the fence so the cut will run along one side of the centerline on the rail (Fig. 1).

4 Slide the rail against the fence along the table-saw deck until it touches the blade. Mark this spot on table-saw deck and fence so they are visible when the rail is passing over the blade. This is where the blade

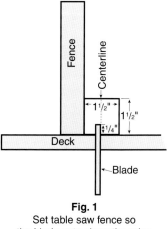

Fig. 1
Set table saw fence so
the blade cuts along the edge
of the centerline ¼" deep.

begins its cut. Repeat at the opposite end of the blade to indicate where the blade cut ends. Again, mark the fence and the deck where it is visible over and to the side of the rail.

5 Make one pass over the table-saw blade with a rail, then turn the rail around with the same edge against the table-saw deck as before and make a second pass to make a ¼x¼-inch dado the full length of the rail. Dry-fit the dado over a scrap piece of the ¼-inch lauan. Adjust if necessary, then cut dadoes in the remaining three rails in the same manner.

PROJECT SIZE
One panel: 26½x1½x72 inches

TOOLS
■ Miter saw
■ Table saw
■ Random orbit sander with 80-sandpaper
■ Plunge router with ⅜-inch roundover and/or Roman ogee bit (optional) plus ¼ inch straight bit and edge guide
■ Drill with screwdriver bit, and ⅛- and ⅜-inch bullet bits

SUPPLIES
■ ¼-inch lauan: 4x8-foot sheet
■ 2x2 pine: four 8-foot lengths
■ Wood glue (optional)
■ Eight 3-inch screws
■ Eight ⅜-inch birch plugs
■ Two 2½-inch brass hinges
■ 220-grit sandpaper
■ Hunter green exterior latex satin paint
■ Minwax semigloss polyurethane

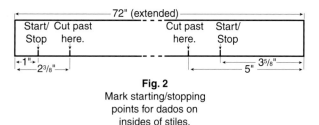

Fig. 2
Mark starting/stopping
points for dados on
insides of stiles.

6 Referring to Fig. 2, measure along the inside edge of each stile and mark both the front and the back at 1 inch and 2⅜ inches from the top and 3⅝ inches and 5 inches from the bottom.

7 Mark each stile 1 inch from the top and 3⅝ inches from the bottom. These are the starting and stopping points for the dadoes. With the ¼-inch straight bit in the plunge router and the router edge guide set so that the dado is centered in the stile, cut the dado between the two marks in each stile.

ASSEMBLE & FINISH

1 Turn all four stiles dado-sides down and top ends together. Measure and mark 1¾ inches from the top and 4¼ inches from the bottom; cross-mark these marks ¾ inch from the side. Predrill a ⅛-inch hole at each of these cross marks. Change to the ⅜-inch bit and drill a ⅜-inch-deep countersink hole at the same point.

2 Dry-assemble the frame rails into one of the side stiles with the top of the top rail at the 1-inch mark and the top of the bottom rail at the 5-inch mark. Drive a 3-inch screw through each predrilled hole into the end of the rail. Slide the lauan panel into the rail dadoes and then into the stile dado. Finish the assembly by adding the remaining stile and securing the two rails at the predrilled locations with the lauan held in the stile dado. Note any adjustments to be made.

3 Dry-assemble the second panel in the same manner. Note adjustments needed.

4 Stack the panels so the backs are together. Mark the hinge locations at 12 inches from the top and 12 inches from the bottom. Install the hinges, beginning at these marks. Disassemble the panels and make the necessary adjustments.

5 With the 80-grit sandpaper in the sander, smooth out all sides of each frame piece. Slightly round over the corners of the frame with the sander. *Note: If more flair is desired, reassemble the frame (without the panel) and detail the frame with the Roman ogee bit, or round the edges with the ⅜-inch roundover bit.*

6 Stain or paint the panel and frame as desired following manufacturer's instructions. For the model, the panel is painted with exterior latex *hunter green* and the frame is natural.

7 Assemble panels and frames. Glue the rails in place if desired. Remove excess glue immediately.

8 Brush on one coat of polyurethane and let dry. Lightly sand with 220-grit sandpaper. Glue the birch plugs in place and apply a second coat of polyurethane.

9 Reinstall the hinges. ●

EASY ROLLING GARDEN CART

Design by Anna Thompson

Big rubber tires make this yard and garden cart easy to roll over bumpy ground.

Note: *All screws are countersunk.*

CUTTING

1 Referring to cutting chart (page 75) for ¾-inch marine-grade plywood, cut two 11⅞x32-inch sides (A), one 24x 32-inch bottom (B), one 11⅞x22¾-inch back (D) and one 9x12-inch drop (F).

2 From the ¾x¾-inch hardwood, cut four 11-inch lengths for back guides (C).

3 From the ⅞x1⅝-inch poplar, cut two 32-inch lengths for handles (H).

4 From the 1⅛x2½-inch poplar, cut two 9-inch lengths for axle

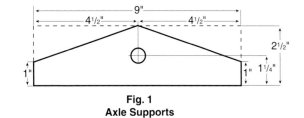

Fig. 1
Axle Supports

supports (E). Referring to Fig. 1, on each axle support, measure 1 inch from the bottom on each end and mark the center at the top; connect the lines from the top center out to the bottom 1-inch marks; cut the angles. Cross-mark the center of each axle support: 4½ inches from each edge and 1¼ inches from the bottom; drill a ⅝-inch hole at this point.

5 Cut the bottom corners of the 9x12-inch drop (F) at 45-degree angles 2-inches from the bottom edge (Fig. 2).

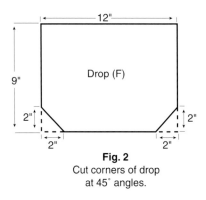

Drop (F)

Fig. 2
Cut corners of drop at 45° angles.

PROJECT SIZE
48x36x21⅝ inches, including wheels

TOOLS
- Table saw or circular saw
- Miter saw
- Drill with ⅛-inch pilot, ⅜-inch countersink and ⅝-inch spade bits

SUPPLIES
- ¾-inch marine-grade plywood: 4x4 feet
- ¾x¾-inch hardwood*: 4 feet
- ⅞x1⅝-inch poplar*: one 8-foot length
- 1⅛x2½-inch poplar*: 24 inches
- 2x6-inch hardwood: 8 inches

- Scrap cardboard
- ⅝-inch threaded rod: 36 inches
- Four ⅝-inch inside diameter bolts
- Two 15-inch-diameter rubber wheel-barrow wheels
- Four 2-inch fender washers
- Two ⅝-inch lock nuts
- 1⅝- and 2-inch wood or drywall screws
- Exterior grade wood glue
- ⅜-inch flush plugs
- Exterior-grade primer
- Exterior-grade paint

*Measurements given are actual, not nominal. Standard nominal lumber will need to be ripped and/or planed to size.

ASSEMBLY DIAGRAM

P	T	W	L	#
A	¾"	11⅞"	32"	2
B	¾"	24"	32"	1
C	¾"	¾"	11"	4
D	¾"	11⅞"	22¾"	1
E	1⅛"	2½"	9"	2
F	¾"	9"	12"	1
G	1½"	5½"	7"	1
H	⅞"	1⅝"	32"	2

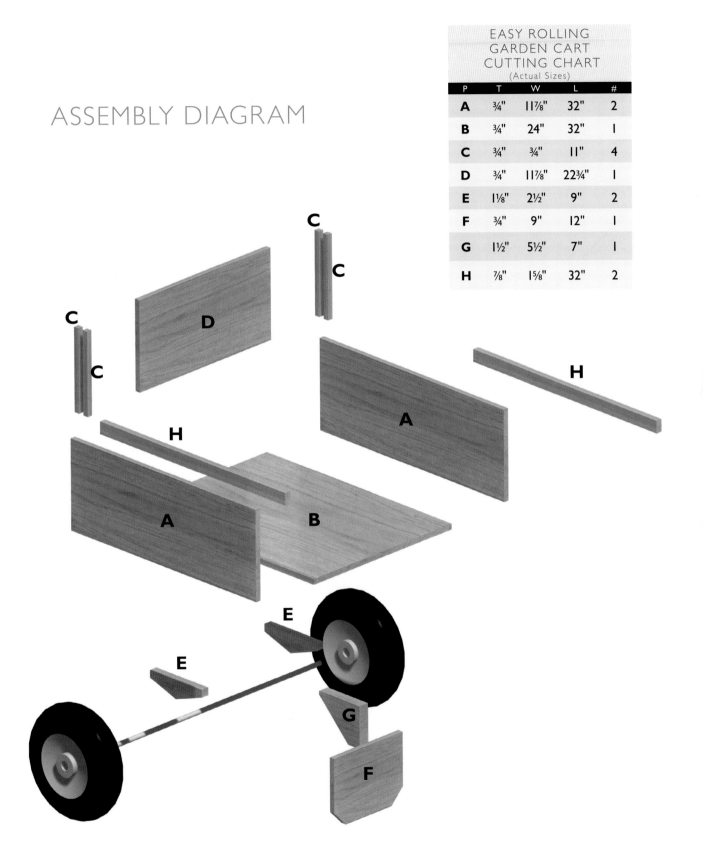

6 At the top of the 2x6, measure and mark 7 inches from one end. At the bottom, measure and mark 1½ inches from the same end. Referring to Fig. 3, draw a line between the two marks and cut for the drop back support (G).

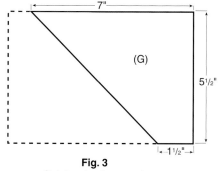

Fig. 3
Cut drop back support.

ASSEMBLY

1 Glue the sides (A) to the bottom (B) flush at the ends and the outside edge; drive 1⅝-inch screws through the bottom into the ends of the sides.

2 Place two of the back guides (C) butted into the bottom (B) and flush with the back edge of each side (A). Glue and screw in place.

3 Slide the back (D) in place against the installed guides. Place the cardboard scraps against the back, then place the remaining two back guides against the cardboard strips. Attach the guides to the sides with glue and 1⅝-inch screws. Remove the back and cardboard; let glue set.

4 Referring to Fig. 4, measure 2 inches from the back edge and 1½ inches from the sides of the bottom (B). Glue and screw the axle supports (E) in place using 2-inch screws driven into the axle supports through the bottom.

5 Center the 5½-inch edge of the drop back support (G) against the back of the drop (F), flush at the top. Secure with glue and 1⅝-inch screws driven through the drop (F) into the end of the drop back support (G).

6 Place the drop unit (F and G) 6 inches from each side and 3½ inches from the front edge. Secure with glue and 2-inch screws driven into the unit from the bottom.

7 Run the ⅝-inch threaded rod through the axle supports (E) centered from side to side. Run two bolts on each side with one against the axle support and the second tight against the first, then slip on a fender washer, a wheel, a fender washer and a lock nut.

8 Attach the handles (H) flush with the tops of the sides and overlapping onto the sides by 16 inches.

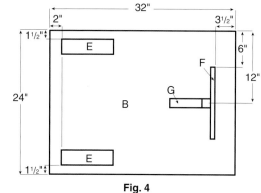

Fig. 4
Bottom Layout

Secure with glue and 1⅝-inch screws driven into the handle through the inside of the cart.

FINISH

1 Glue flush plugs in all countersunk screw holes; let dry. Sand flush.

2 Remove the wheels. Apply exterior-grade primer, then top-coat with paint. *Note: Finish the back prior to placement between the guides.*

3 Reattach the wheels. Slide the back in place. ●

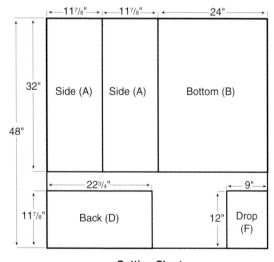

Cutting Chart
¾" Marine-Grade Plywood

SUMMER COTTAGE CURIO

Design by Patti J. Ryan

This dual-shelf display unit has gently curving sides reminiscent of a row boat.

CUTTING

1 From the ½-inch plywood, cut two 10x23½-inch pieces for curio front and back, three 7¾x8-inch pieces for shelves, two 10x7-inch pieces for base plates, twelve 1½x7-inch pieces for side spacers and one 1x7-inch piece for peak spacer.

2 For full-size pattern, cut arch pattern from folded paper, extending sides so total height of pattern is 23½ inches. Transfer pattern to the 10x23½-inch front piece. Clamp the curio back to curio front; cut inside and outside edges of arch with jigsaw.

3 From the ¼-inch plywood, cut one 9½x23-inch piece for backing board. To rout the vertical grooves in the backing board, set the router fence so the tip of the V-groove bit is exactly at the center of the 9½-inch width. With the ¼-inch V-groove bit set to cut ⅛ inch deep, make one pass. Move the router table fence 1 inch, and make one pass with each side against the fence. Move the fence 1 inch after each cut and make one pass with each side until all the vertical grooves are routed. ***Note:*** *Always keep the same side of the backing board against the router-table deck.*

4 Place the curio front on the face side of the backer board, flush at the top; trace the outside of the arch. Cutting to the inside of the traced line, cut the arch in the backer board.

5 From the ⅛-inch bendable plywood, cut two 8x22⅞-inch pieces for inside wraps and two 8x26-inch pieces for outside wraps.

6 Sand all cut edges smooth with sanding pad or disk sander.

PROJECT SIZE
11½xx8¾x23½ inches

TOOLS
- Table saw
- Clamps
- Jigsaw or band saw
- Router with table and ¼-inch V-groove bit
- Bench disk sander
- Carpenter's square
- Utility knife
- Miter saw
- Nail set
- Stapler or brad nailer (optional)
- Drill

SUPPLIES
- ½-inch paintable plywood: 36x36 inches
- ¼-inch paintable plywood: 12x24 inches
- ⅛-inch bendable plywood: 36x36 inches
- ¾x1½-inch trim molding: 30 inches
- Wood glue
- Nails: ⅝-inch brad, ¾-inch finish and 1-inch common
- 80-grit sandpaper
- Paintable wood filler
- 220-grit wet/dry sandpaper
- DecoArt Americana Satins Primer & Stain Blocker #DSA34 and satin varnish #DSA27
- DecoArt Americana Satins acrylic paint: soft natural, #DSA40, buttercream #DSA03
- DecoArt Americana Gloss Spray Sealer #DAS12
- Hanging hardware (optional)

ASSEMBLE

Note: *Refer to assembly diagram throughout.*

1 Determine which of the curio front and back pieces will be the outside of the curio and mark them for orientation. Measure from the bottom and mark 2½, 7, 8½, 10, 15½, 17, 18½ and 22 inches. Set the curio back piece next to the curio front piece so the bottoms are flush and transfer the lines to both edges, and inside and outside surfaces of both frames.

2 Glue and nail the two 10x7-inch base plates together flat and flush with the bottom of curio front and back and the outside edges.

3 Center the ½x1x7-inch top spacer at the peak, flush at the bottom. Mark the angle of the peak on the ends and use the disk sander to file down the spacer to match. Glue and brad nail to curio front and back. Glue and nail inside spacers to curio front and back, flush to the inside, as shown in diagram. **Note:** *If necessary, use a spacer to keep the peak straight while glue dries.*

4 Dry-fit the inside wraps of the bendable plywood. Mark excess and trim, using a utility knife and carpenter's square. Add glue to the frames and spacers, and secure inside wraps one side at a time with brad nails, beginning at the bottom spacer and working toward the top.

5 Glue bottom shelf in place on top of base plate, secure with 1-inch nails driven through the spacers into the ends of the shelf. Secure the second and third shelves in the same manner so the shelf bottoms are 9 and 16 inches from the bottom of the frame.

6 Glue and nail the outside spacers in place as shown in diagram. Dry-fit the outside wraps of the bendable plywood; mark and trim in same manner as for inside wraps. Add glue to the frames and spacers and secure outside wraps one side at a time with brad nails, beginning at the bottom of the sides and working toward the top.

7 Sand surfaces with the sanding pad. Fill nail holes and gaps with wood filler.

8 Cut trim molding with mitered corners to fit around bottom front and sides. Predrill holes and attach with glue and ¾-inch finish nails.

9 Set nails and fill with wood filler. Let dry and sand flush. Remove dust.

FINISHING

1 Following manufacturer's instructions, apply primer to all surfaces, including the grooved side of the backer board.

2 **Note:** *Apply two coats of paint, letting dry after each coat.* Paint shelves and inside wrap with *soft natural;* paint all outside surfaces and primed backer board with *buttercream.*

3 Using glue and 1-inch common nails, attach backer board to back with grooved side facing the front. Let dry.

4 Apply a coat of satin varnish following manufacturer's instructions; let dry. Lightly wet-sand with 220-grit sandpaper, wipe clean and dry, then apply the second coat. Let dry. Spray with several light coats of gloss sealer.

5 If desired, attach hanging hardware. ●

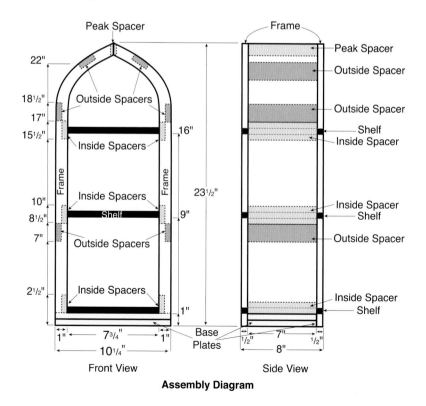

Assembly Diagram

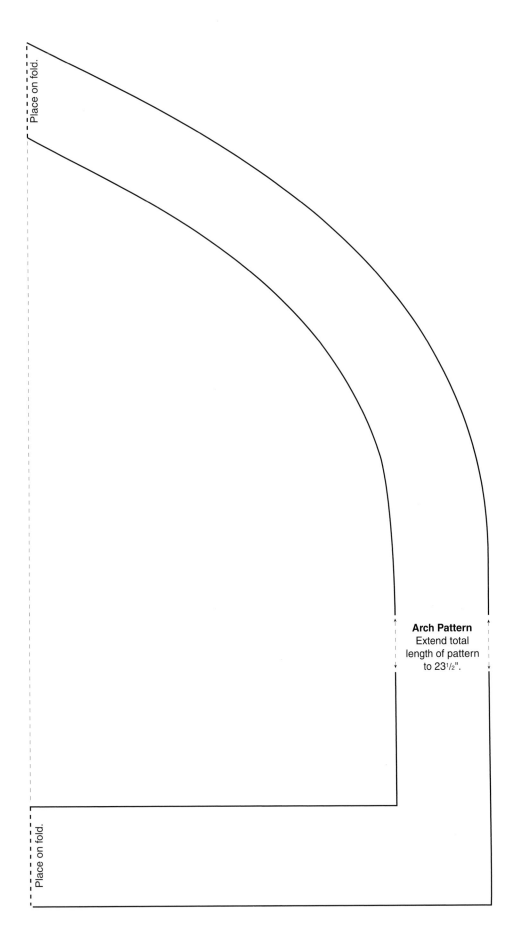

Place on fold.

Place on fold.

Arch Pattern
Extend total
length of pattern
to 23 1/2".

Ahoy, matey! Keep chilled beverages close at hand on your porch or patio with this seafaring cooler and serving-tray set.

PROJECT SIZE
23x23x16½ inches, excluding casters

TOOLS
- Craft knife
- Table saw
- Large compass, or string, pushpin and pencil
- Jigsaw or band saw
- Drill with ¾-inch spade bit and screw driver bits
- Bench disk sander
- Carpenter's square
- Nail set
- Staple gun or brad nailer (optional)

SUPPLIES
- ⅛-inch bendable plywood: 4x8-foot sheet (grain running with 48-inch side)
- ½-inch paintable plywood: 4x4-foot sheet
- 9x12-inch stencil blank
- Black fine-point permanent marker
- Wood glue
- Fasteners: ⅝-inch brads, 1-inch finish nails and #6 ½-inch wood screws
- Paintable wood filler
- Sanding pad with 80-grit sandpaper
- 220-grit wet/dry sandpaper
- DecoArt Americana Satins Primer & Stain Blocker #DSA34
- DecoArt Americana Satins acrylic paint: white satin #DSA01
- DecoArt Americana acrylic paint: baby blue #DA042 and sapphire #DA099
- DecoArt Americana Satins satin varnish #DSA28
- Krylon silver leafing pen
- DecoArt Americana Gloss Spray Sealer #DAS12
- Four 1⅝-inch swivel casters with screw-on plates
- Six stainless steel two-hole open-base boat cleats
- Four clear self-adhesive acrylic pads
- White three-strand twisted polypropylene rope: 10 feet of ½-inch, and 5 feet of ⅛-inch
- 5-gallon painter's bucket with handle
- Four 15-inch white boat fenders

STENCIL
1 Place stencil blank over stencil pattern; trace pattern with permanent marker.

2 Using a sharp craft knife, cut out stencil.

CUTTING
1 Using the table saw, rip the ⅛-inch bendable plywood the full length (96 inches) into one 16½-inch strip for outside wrap, one 16-inch strip for inside wrap and one 1¾-inch strip for tray edge.

2 Cut the 16½-inch outside wrap to 66 inches, the 16-inch inside wrap to 50 inches and the 1¾-inch tray edge to 48 inches.

3 Using the table saw, cut the ½-inch plywood in half, then cut one length in half again making two 2x2-foot pieces and one 2x4-foot piece.

4 Rip the 2x4-foot ½-inch plywood to 15½x48 inches. Reset the table-saw fence to 2⅜ inches and rip twelve 2⅜x15½-inch vertical supports.

5 Using the large compass, or the string/pushpin combination, draw

a 21-inch-diameter (10½-inch-radius) circle on one 2x2-foot piece, then draw a 16-inch-diameter (8-inch-radius) circle and a 15¼-inch-diameter (7⅝-inch-radius) circle inside the first circle, using the same center points.

6 Stack and clamp both 2x2-foot pieces together and cut out the 21-inch circle from both pieces. Separate the boards, set the unmarked circle aside for the bottom, then cut the 16-inch-diameter circle from the remaining circle (waste is to the inside) to make the top rim. Cut the 15¼-inch circle (waste is to the outside) from the cutout portion of the top rim for the tray base.

7 Drill three drainage holes 4 inches from the center in the bottom plywood circle using the ¾-inch spade bit.

8 Smooth out the edges of the circles with the disk sander or sanding pad.

BASE ASSEMBLY

1 Stack the top rim on the bottom circle. Trace inside the rim onto the bottom for inner-assembly guideline. Divide and mark the top rim and bottom into twelve identical sections. Using the carpenter's square, continue these marks onto the outside edges of both circles and to the inside rim (Fig. 1).

2 Position the twelve vertical supports at these marks. Secure supports to the top rim and the bottom with wood glue and 1-inch nails driven into the ends of the support through the top rim and the bottom.

3 Dry-fit the inside wrap by rolling it up and sliding it inside the top rim.

The wrap should be flush at the top when resting on the bottom.

4 Mark the ends where they overlap, then remove the wrap and cut to the mark with craft knife and carpenter's square. Add wood glue along inside rim and vertical supports, then set the wrap back inside the rim, making sure the splice is on one of the vertical supports. Secure to the rim with four or five brads.

5 In a similar manner, fit and trim the outside wrap around the outside of the top rim, bottom and supports; and secure it with glue and brads into rim and bottom.

6 Set nails with the nail set, then fill holes with paintable wood filler. Let dry.

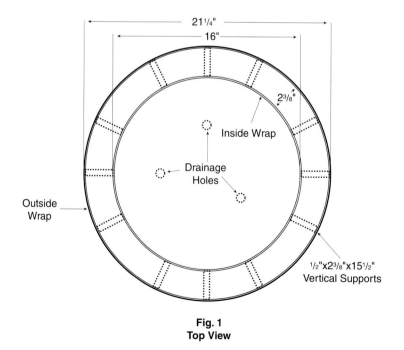

**Fig. 1
Top View**

7 Sand outside wrap flush to the bottom. Remove excess wood filler, then wipe clean.

TRAY ASSEMBLY

1 Wrap the tray edge around the 15¼-inch tray base; mark the overlap and trim with utility knife.

2 Position tray strip to the tray base so it is flush at the bottom; attach with glue and brads.

3 Lightly sand the top of the tray edge to round over the edges. Sand the bottom of the tray edge flush with the tray base.

FINISH

1 Apply primer and stain blocker to all surfaces of base and tray; let dry 30 minutes, then coat again. Lightly

wet-sand with 220-grit sandpaper, then wipe clean and dry. Apply two coats of *white satin* to all surfaces, letting dry after each coat. Apply two coats of satin varnish to all surfaces. Lightly wet-sand with 220-grit sandpaper; wipe clean, and let dry completely.

2 Using ½-inch screws, predrill holes and anchor a boat cleat on every third support on the caddy sides, 2 inches from the top.

3 Tape stencil in place between cleats. Load stencil brush with *baby blue* and remove most of the paint on a paper towel. Apply paint with small swirling strokes, working from the stencil edge inward. In same manner, apply *sapphire* to the outer edges of the stencil only. Remove stencil and reposition to repeat process on base

three more times and once on the tray center. Add rope detail to each stencil using silver leafing pen.

4 Seal caddy base and tray with several coats of gloss spray sealer.

FINAL ASSEMBLY

1 Add the casters with ½-inch screws 1 inch from the outside edge and in line with each boat cleat.

2 Attach two boat cleats for tray handles to the top of tray base with ½-inch screws 2 inches from the sides and directly opposite each other. Add clear self-adhesive acrylic pads to bottom of tray base.

3 Loop and swag the ½-inch rope between the boat cleats and secure the ends with a square knot. Cut off excess and tie off the ends with pieces of ¼-inch rope; seal knots with a dab of glue. For the ¼-inch rope, tie off ends and secure with a dab of glue.

4 Cut four 12-inch lengths of ⅛-inch rope. Loop each length through the end of the boat fender and tie to a cleat.

5 Insert the 5-gallon bucket in the base. Rest tray on top of bucket (Fig. 2). To use, load cold drinks and ice in the bucket then set it in the base. The tray can be used separately. Store out of the weather when not in use. ●

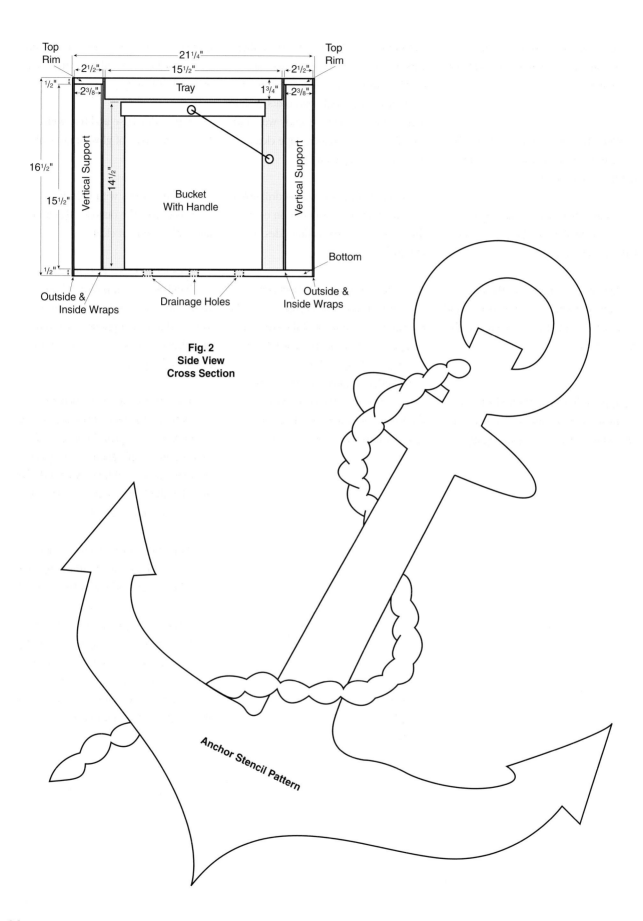

Top Rim

Top Rim

21¼"

15½"

2½"

2½"

½"

2⅜"

Tray

1¾"

2⅜"

Vertical Support

14½"

Vertical Support

16½"

15½"

Bucket
With Handle

Bottom

½"

Outside &
Inside Wraps

Drainage Holes

Outside &
Inside Wraps

Fig. 2
Side View
Cross Section

Anchor Stencil Pattern

SIMPLE PORCH PLANTER

Design by Barbara Greve

Clean lines and easy construction make a welcome addition to a sheltered porch or patio.

CUTTING

1 Rip and cut the oak plywood into four 8x11-inch sides. Iron on oak veneer edging to one 11-inch edge of each, then trim off excess. On the inside of each side, drill two pocket holes on each end to attach to legs.

2 From the 2x3-inch pine, cut four 22-inch legs.

3 From the 1x2 pine, cut two 16-inch lower slat supports, six 15-inch upper slats and six 11-inch lower slats.

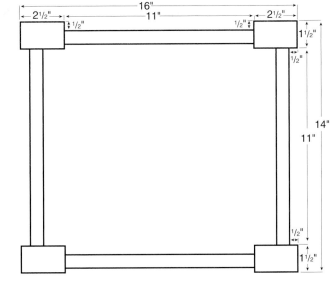

Fig. 1
Side/Leg Assembly
Top View

PROJECT SIZE
16x14x22 inches

TOOLS
- Table saw
- Veneer trimmer
- Pocket-hole jig
- Drill with ⁷⁄₆₄- and ¼-inch bits
- Miter saw (optional)
- Clamps, including right-angle clamp
- Sander with 120- to 320-grit sandpaper

SUPPLIES
- ¾-inch oak plywood*: 24x48 inches
- 2x3-inch pine**: two 48-inch lengths
- 1x2 pine: one 36-inch and four 4-foot lengths
- ¾-inch iron-on oak veneer edging: 4 feet
- Wood glue
- 1¼-inch coarse-thread pocket-hole screws
- 1-inch brads
- 1-inch wood or drywall screws
- Pocket-hole plugs
- Wood filler
- DecoArt Americana Satins acrylic paint: sage green #DSA21, antique gold #DSA41 and dark ecru #DSA06
- DecoArt DuraClear satin varnish #DS21

*Paint-grade birch plywood and veneer edging may be substituted for the oak.

**Measurements given are actual, not nominal. Standard nominal lumber will need to be ripped and/or planed to size.

ASSEMBLE & FINISH

1 Position each side ½ inch from the outside edge of the legs and ¾ inch from the top (Fig. 1) and clamp in place; attach with glue and pocket-hole screws. Remove clamps.

2 Turn planter upside down. Position six 15-inch upper slats evenly spaced across the bottom of the planter flush at the outside edges; attach ends of slats to sides with glue and 1-inch brads.

3 Lay the planter on one long (16-inch) side. Position one 16-inch lower slat support to the legs beginning 2 inches from the bottom. Using the ¼-inch bit, predrill and countersink holes, then secure support with glue and a 1-inch screw in each end. Turn the planter onto the other 16-inch side and repeat to attach the other lower slat support.

4 Stand planter upright. Position six 11-inch lower slats evenly spaced across the lower slat supports; attach in same manner as upper slats (step 2).

5 Glue pocket-hole plugs in place; fill gaps and holes with wood filler. Let dry, then sand smooth and remove dust.

6 Mix equal parts *sage green, dark ecru* and *antique gold*. Apply at least two coats to planter letting dry and sanding with 320-grit sandpaper between coats. Let dry.

7 Apply at least two coats of satin varnish to seal, following manufacturer's instructions. ●

CHECKERBOARD FLOWER TABLE

Design by Loretta Mateik

This fanciful flower-shaped table brings lots of style to small spaces.

CUTTING

1 Using patterns provided for table base and table top, make full-size patterns as indicated. Transfer outlines and center marks to ¾-inch plywood.

2 Cut out the table base with the table saw; cut out the table top with the scroll saw.

3 Cut the 1⅜-inch dowel to 22 inches. Drill a ¹⁄₁₆-inch hole in the center of each end of the dowel rod.

4 Drill a ⅛-inch pilot hole through the centers of table top and table base. Using ⅜-inch countersink bit, countersink holes on top of table top and bottom of table base.

5 Change to the 1⅜-inch Forstner bit. On the center bottom of the table top and the center top of the table base, drill a ½-inch-deep hole.

6 Sand pieces smooth; wipe clean.

ASSEMBLE & FINISH

1 Seal pieces with a light coat of varnish, let dry. Sand lightly again and wipe clean.

2 Base-coat dowel and table base with *Hauser dark green*. Base-coat both sides of table top with *burnt orange*. Let dry. Transfer pattern detail to top of table top.

3 Paint flower petals with *burnt sienna*. **Note:** *Apply a second coat if needed.*

4 Add *burnt orange* to *burnt sienna* to lighten; stencil checkerboard pattern onto table top. Let dry.

5 Outline petals with *lamp black*.

6 Glue dowel rod into 1⅜-inch holes in table top and table base; secure with a 2-inch drywall screw through predrilled hole through base and top into ends of dowel. Remove excess glue immediately; let dry.

7 Fill screw hole in table top with wood filler so a minimal amount of sanding is needed. Let dry, then sand and wipe clean.

8 Using photo as a guide, paint center of table top with *dark chocolate* to cover filler; apply a second

PROJECT SIZE
11¼x11¼x22½ inches

TOOLS
- Table saw with miter gauge
- Scroll saw
- Drill with 1⅜-inch Forstner bit, ¹⁄₁₆- and ⅛-inch bits, and ⅜-inch countersink bit

SUPPLIES
- ¾-inch plywood: 12x48 inches
- 1⅜-inch closet-rod dowel: 24 inches
- 220-grit sandpaper
- Multi-purpose satin varnish
- DecoArt Americana acrylic paints: burnt orange #DA016, burnt sienna #DA063, Hauser dark green #DA133, lamp black #DA067 and dark chocolate #DA065
- 1-inch checkerboard stencil
- Wood glue
- Two 2-inch drywall screws
- Wood filler

coat if needed. Outline center flower with *lamp black.*

9 Remove visible pattern lines. Apply several light coats of satin varnish, following manufacturer's directions. ●

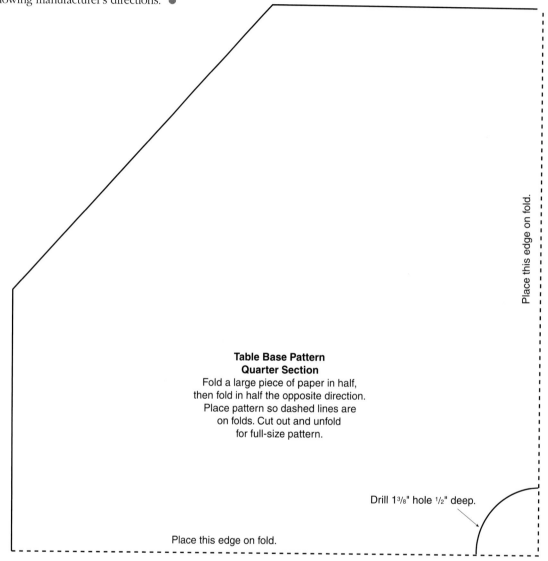

Place this edge on fold.

Table Base Pattern
Quarter Section
Fold a large piece of paper in half,
then fold in half the opposite direction.
Place pattern so dashed lines are
on folds. Cut out and unfold
for full-size pattern.

Drill 1³/₈" hole ¹/₂" deep.

Place this edge on fold.

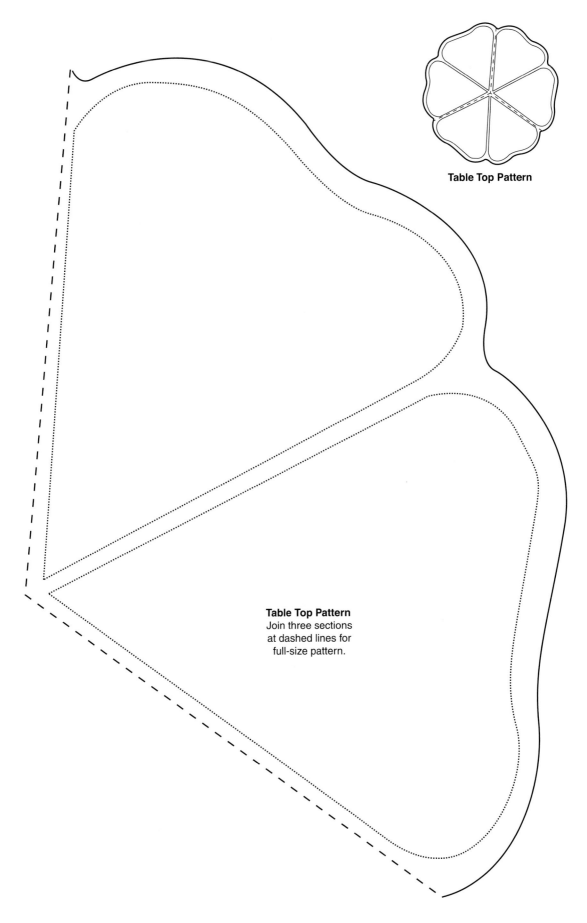

Table Top Pattern

Table Top Pattern
Join three sections
at dashed lines for
full-size pattern.

PETITE PASTEL TABLE

Design by Barbara Greve

This little color-washed table fits almost anywhere—at the bedside, next to a chair or tucked in a corner.

CUTTING

1 Rip and cut the ¾-inch oak plywood to make two 10x18¼-inch sides, one 11x22-inch tabletop and one 6½x18⁷⁄₁₆-inch shelf.

2 Clamp the two side pieces together. Lightly mark the vertical center across one side piece and transfer the curve pattern as indicated on the pattern. Use a jigsaw to cut the curves through both sides at the same time. Sand out saw marks.

ASSEMBLE & FINISH

1 Band the perimeter of the tabletop and the long sides of the shelf and side pieces with the ¾-inch oak veneer iron-on edge tape.

2 Following manufacturer's instructions, use the pocket hole jig to drill three holes on the inside top edge of each side piece for attaching the top; drill two holes on the underside of the shelf at each end for attaching to sides.

3 Place one side piece on the work surface with inside facing up. Lightly draw a line across the side 5½ inches from the bottom. Apply glue to end of shelf and position the bottom of the shelf along this line and centered in the width of the side; clamp in place and drive in 1¼-inch pocket-hole screws. Attach opposite end of shelf to remaining side in the same manner.

4 Place tabletop facedown on the work surface. Apply glue to top of sides and center sides/shelf unit on tabletop; clamp in place and drive in 1¼-inch pocket-hole screws. Let dry. Remove clamps.

5 Glue pocket-hole plugs in place and fill holes or gaps with wood filler. Sand flush and smooth; remove dust.

Note: *Apply two coats of paint, letting dry and sanding lightly with 320-grit sandpaper between coats.*

6 Mix equal parts *buttercream* with *soft white.* Apply two coats to top and bottom of the tabletop and shelf. Let dry.

PROJECT SIZE
22x11x19 inches

TOOLS
- Table saw
- Jigsaw
- Sander with 80-, 120- and 320-grit sandpaper
- Edge trimmer
- Pocket-hole jig
- Drill
- Clamps: right angle and others

SUPPLIES
- ¾-inch oak veneer plywood: 24x48 inches
- ¾-inch oak veneer iron-on edge tape, approximately 15 feet
- 1¼-inch coarse-thread pocket-hole screws
- Pocket-hole plugs
- Wood glue
- Wood filler
- DecoArt Americana Satins acrylic paint: sage green #DSA21, French blue #DSA43, soft white #DSA02, buttercream #DSA03
- DecoArt DuraClear satin varnish #DS21

7 Mix equal parts *sage green* and *soft white.* Apply two coats to inside and outside of side pieces. Let dry.

8 Apply two coats of *French blue* to edges of top, sides and shelf. Let dry.

9 Apply two coats of satin varnish following manufacturer's instructions. ●

Horizontal Centerline

Vertical Centerline

Curve Pattern
Align vertical centerline and bottom edge of pattern with vertical centerline and bottom edge of side to transfer curve and horizontal centerline to bottom left quadrant.
Flip pattern up, aligning horizontal centerlines, vertical centerlines and top edges to transfer curve to upper left quadrant.
Flip pattern over and transfer curve to right quadrants in same manner.

Bottom/Top Edge

CHEERY CHILDREN'S BENCH

Design by Barbara Greve

Build a sunny yellow bench for a special child. There's even room for favorite books or treasured toys.

CUTTING

1 From the ½-inch plywood, cut one 17x22-inch piece for bench back.

2 From the ¾-inch plywood, cut two 10¼x9½-inch pieces for bench sides, and two 10¼x20½-inch pieces for bench top and bottom.

3 With the ¼-inch roundover bit, rout all four edges of the 2x2-inch pine; cut into four 2-inch lengths for feet.

4 Transfer the bench back-corner pattern to bench back as indicated on pattern; cut with jigsaw. Smooth out roughness of the cuts with the sander and 120-grit sandpaper.

5 Set the pocket-hole jig collar for ¾-inch stock; in the bottom of the bench top and bottom boards, drill two pocket holes in each end for attaching sides. Drill one pocket hole into each foot for attaching to bench bottom.

6 Reset the collar for ½-inch stock; drill two pocket holes at the back bottom long edge of bench top and bottom for attaching bench back.

7 Sand rough areas smooth and remove dust.

ASSEMBLE & FINISH

1 With a dry iron set on cotton, iron on the oak veneer edging to exposed plywood edges; trim excess. Fill gaps or holes with wood filler; let dry, then sand smooth and remove dust.

2 *Note: Refer to bench assembly diagram on page 99 for assembly.* Spread glue on ends of bench top and bottom; attach to bench sides with 1¼-inch pocket-hole screws through the predrilled holes. Let dry.

3 Spread glue on back edges of bench top, bottom and sides; position the bench back, centered side to side and flush at the bottom, then attach with 1-inch pocket-hole screws. Let dry.

4 Turn the bench upside down (the top of the back will hang off the

PROJECT SIZE
22x10¾x19 inches

TOOLS
- Table saw
- Router and router table with ¼-inch roundover bit
- Jigsaw
- Pocket-hole jig
- Drill
- Sander with 120- and 320-grit sandpaper
- Veneer trimmer

SUPPLIES
- ½-inch oak plywood*: 24x24 inches
- ¾-inch oak plywood*: 24x48 inches
- 2x2-inch pine: 12 inches
- ¾-inch oak veneer iron-on edging*: approximately 9 feet
- Wood filler
- Crafter's Pick Sand-N-Stain glue
- 1¼- and 1-inch pocket-hole screws
- DecoArt Americana Satins acrylic paint: buttercream #DSA03

*Paint-grade birch plywood and veneer edging may be substituted for the oak.

work surface). Measure 1 inch from each front/back edge and ½ inch from each end. Set a pine foot in each corner at these marks and attach with 1¼-inch pocket-hole screws. Let dry.

5 Apply at least two coats of *buttercream,* letting dry and sanding lightly with 320-grit sandpaper between coats. ●

Back
Top
Side
Side
Bottom
3/4"
3/4"
9 1/2"
17"
20 1/2"
22"
3/4"
3/4"
Front View
Back
Top
Side
Bottom
3/4"
9 1/2"
3/4"
1/2"
10 1/4"
Side View

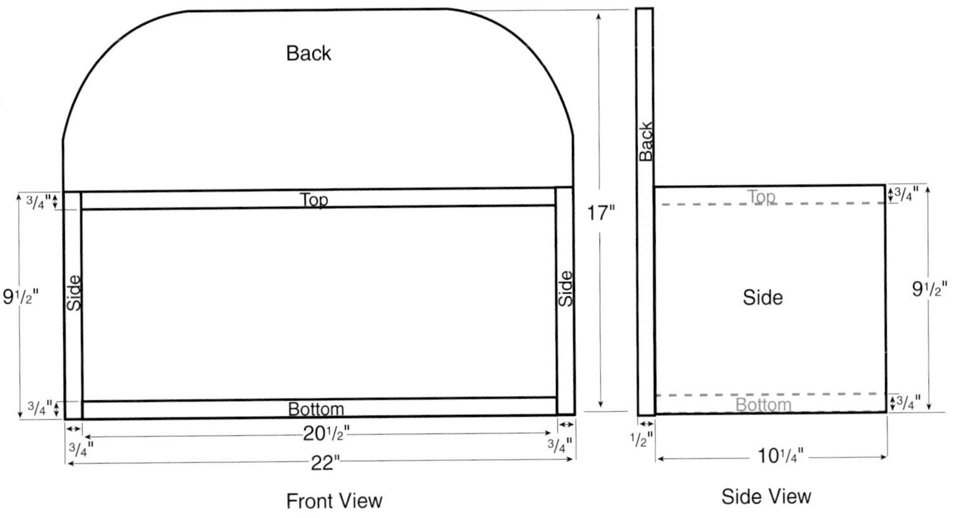

Bench Assembly Diagram

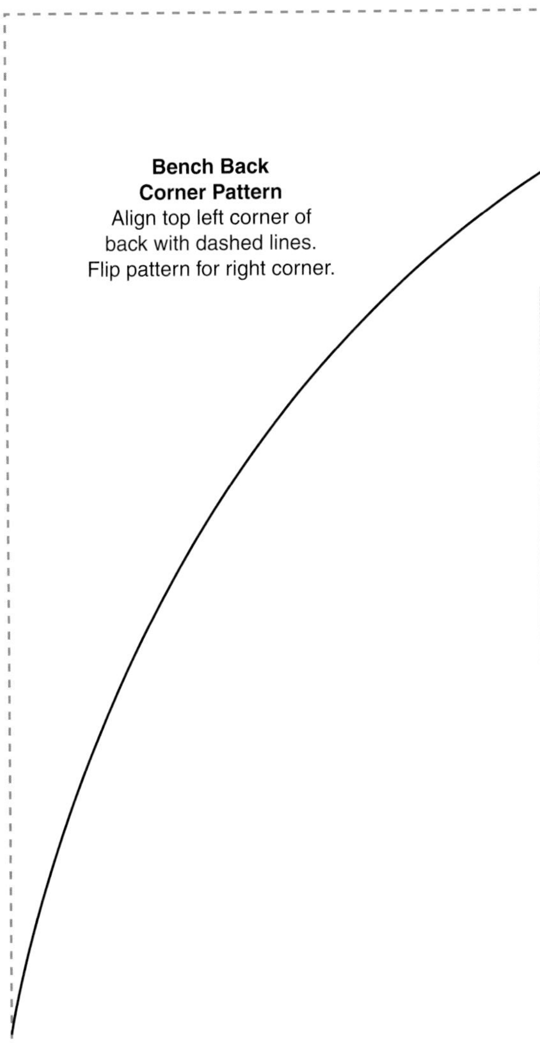

Bench Back
Corner Pattern
Align top left corner of
back with dashed lines.
Flip pattern for right corner.

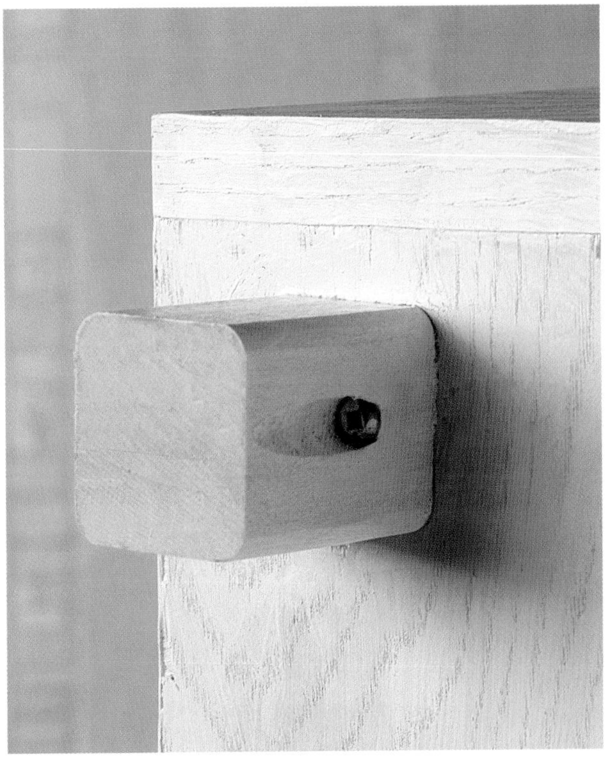

CURVACEOUS PLYWOOD BOWL

Design by Linda Van Gehuchten

A shapely veneer stripe accents a classic turned bowl.

BLANK PREPARATION

1 Using wood glue, glue the four plywood squares together making one 5x5x3-inch block for the turning blank. Clamp tightly and let dry for 2 hours.

2 Draw a line across both diagonals from corner to corner to mark the center.

3 Remove the excess glue from the edges of the turning blank with either the sliding table on the table saw, the miter saw or a combination sander.

Photo I

4 Draw a line across one side of the blank 1¼ inches from what will be

the top. Line up the 10-inch cardboard circle with the outside edge marks and draw the arc. Mark two hash marks across the arc. These will be needed to realign parts in a later step.

5 On the band saw, cut the curved mark on the blank. Do not sand or shape the curves. Remove any dust from cutting.

6 Spread wood glue on both surfaces of the cut blank. Sandwich the black veneer between the two halves, line up the hash marks so the sides will fit back together properly, and clamp. Place the first clamp in the middle and tighten down, then clamp each of the four corners (Photo 1). Let this dry for 2 hours.

PROJECT SIZE
Approximately 5 inches in diameter
   x 2½ inches

TOOLS
- Clamps
- Table saw
- Miter saw
- Combination sander
- Band saw
- Compass
- Lathe with self-centering chuck and worm screw
- Turning tools: ¼- and ½-inch bowl gouges, parting tool and round nosed scraper

- Cordless drill with 80- to 320-grit regular and soft sanding disks

SUPPLIES
- ¾-inch Baltic birch plywood: four 5x5-inch squares
- Black veneer: one 5¼x5¼-inch square
- Titebond Original wood glue
- 10-inch cardboard circle or pie plate
- Latex gloves
- Medium cyanoacrylate (CA) glue
- CA glue aerosol activator
- Deft spray lacquer

7 Unclamp the blank and, using the cross mark of the diagonals as the pivot point, use the compass to draw a 5-inch-diameter circle in the top of the blank. Cut with the band saw.

8 Following manufacturer's instructions, drill a hole the recommended size in the center of the blank for the worm screw. Screw the blank on the worm screw until it meets the face of chuck.

TURNING
Outside of bowl

1 Bring up the tailstock to secure the blank and mark its center.

2 With the beginning lathe speed set at 800 rpm, use the bowl gouge held at a 45-degree angle with the flute facing the work to begin rounding the outside corner (the end toward the tailstock) for the base of the bowl. Begin with short cuts as the corners are cut away. Cuts will become longer as the bowl begins to take shape.

3 For cutting from the rim to the foot, start with the flute facing the direction of the cut (the tailstock). Once contact is made, slightly rotate the flute up, so the sharpest edge of the tool is making the cut.

4 After rounding the bowl blank, make a ¼-inch-long tenon at the foot.

5 Using the cordless drill and sanding disks, sand the outside of the bowl progressively from 80- to 320-grit.

6 Remove the bowl from the worm screw. Determine the depth of the finished bowl and mark this depth on the same bit with which the worm screw hole was drilled. Drill into the blank to the depth marked on the bit.

7 Remove the worm screw from the chuck, then reattach the bowl blank in the chuck with the tenon, making sure it sits flat on the face of the chuck.

Inside of bowl

1 Begin to hollow out the bowl with the bowl gouge. Adjust the tool-rest height so the center of the bowl gouge is cutting just above the center of the bowl. Start about ½ inch from the drilled center hole. Hold the gouge at a 45-degree angle to the surface to be cut, with the flute facing the direction of the cut and the bevel lined up in the direction of the cut.

2 Using the thumb as a stop behind the tool rest, pivot the tool into the blank. Hollowing out the bowl is a successive progression of cuts. Make the cuts as fluid as possible, coming into the wood without letting the centrifugal force kick the tool out.

3 When the rim is reached, cut a groove with the parting tool to define the rim edge, then hollow out to the groove.

4 Use a 2-inch soft sanding disk for the inside; beginning with 80-grit, progress through the grits until the inside is smooth.

FINISH

Caution: *Work in a well-ventilated area and wear a face mask and latex or nitrite gloves.*

1 Due to the end-grains of the plywood, a sealer must be used on the inside of the bowl. Put a drop or two of medium CA glue in the bowl and spread it over the piece. Continue to add glue, one or two drops at a time, until the entire inside of the bowl is coated. Spray with activator.

2 Sand lightly with 320-grit sandpaper.

3 With a waste block on a faceplate, refer to lathe manufacturer's instructions to make a "jam-fit" chuck. Remount the bowl in the lathe securely seated in the jam-fit chuck.

4 Finish shaping the base and turn the bottom of the bowl concave with a small bowl gouge. Sand with the soft-sanding disks.

5 Seal the outside of the bowl in the same manner as the inside. After sanding the bowl with 320-grit sandpaper, spray Deft lacquer on the bowl. ●

TWIST & TURNED PLYWOOD BOWL

Design by Linda Van Gehuchten

A stripe of veneer adds an unexpected twist to a turned plywood bowl.

BLANK PREPARATION

1 Using wood glue, glue the three plywood squares together making one 5x5x2¼-inch block for turning blank. Clamp tightly and let dry for 2 hours.

2 Trace an arc of the cardboard circle at random on the top of the glued squares. Mark two hash marks across the arc. These will be needed to realign parts in a later step.

3 On the band saw, cut the curved mark on the blank. Do not sand or shape the curves. Remove any dust from cutting.

4 Spread wood glue on both surfaces of the turning blank. Sandwich the black veneer between the two halves, making sure hash marks are aligned for a proper fit; clamp. Place the first clamp in the middle and tighten down, then clamp (Photo 1).

5 Draw a line across both diagonals from corner to corner to mark the center. With the compass draw a 5-inch-

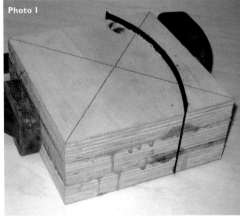

Photo I

diameter circle in the blank. Cut with the band saw.

6 Following the manufacturer's instructions, drill a hole the recommended size in the center of the blank for the worm screw. Screw the blank on the worm screw until it meets the face of chuck.

TURNING
Outside of bowl

1 Bring up the tailstock to secure the blank and mark its center.

2 With the beginning lathe speed set at 800 rpm, use the bowl gouge held at a 45-degree angle with the flute facing the work to begin rounding the outside corner (the end toward the tailstock) for the base of the bowl. Begin with short cuts as the corners are

PROJECT SIZE

Approximately 5 inches in diameter
x 1¾ inches

TOOLS

- Table saw
- Miter saw
- Clamps
- Band saw
- Compass
- Lathe with self-centering chuck and worm screw
- Turning tools: ¼- and ½-inch bowl gouges, parting tool and round-nose scraper
- Cordless drill with 80- through 320-grit sanding disks

SUPPLIES

- ¾-inch Baltic birch plywood: three 5x5-inch squares
- ¹⁄₄₀-inch or thicker black veneer: 5¼x5¼-inch square
- 10-inch cardboard circle or pie plate
- Titebond Original wood glue
- Latex gloves
- Medium Cyanoacylate (CA) glue
- CA glue aerosol activator
- Deft spray lacquer

cut away. Cuts will become longer as the bowl begins to take shape.

3 For cutting from the rim to the foot, start with the flute facing the direction of the cut (the tailstock). Once contact is made, slightly rotate the flute up, so the sharpest edge of the tool is making the cut.

4 After rounding the bowl blank, make a ¼-inch-long tenon at the foot.

5 Using the cordless drill and sanding disks, sand the outside of the bowl progressively from 80- to 320-grit.

6 Remove the bowl from the worm screw. Mark the depth of the bowl by drilling into the blank the determined depth of the bowl using the bit used to predrill the worm screw hole.

7 Remove the worm screw from the chuck, then reattach the bowl blank in the chuck with the tenon, making sure it sits flat on the face of the chuck.

Inside of bowl

1 Begin to hollow out the bowl with the bowl gouge. Adjust the tool-rest height so the center of the bowl gouge is cutting just above the center of the bowl. Start about ½ inch from the drilled center hole. Hold the gouge at a 45-degree angle to the surface to be cut, with the flute facing the direction of the cut and the bevel lined up in the direction of the cut.

2 Using the thumb as a stop behind the tool rest, pivot the tool into the blank. Hollowing out the bowl is a successive progression of cuts. Make the cuts as fluid as possible, coming into the wood without letting the centrifugal force kick the tool out.

3 When the rim is reached, cut a groove with the parting tool to define the rim edge, then hollow out to the groove.

4 Use a 2-inch soft sanding disk for the inside, beginning with 80-grit and progress through the grits until the inside is smooth.

FINISH

Caution: *Work in a well-ventilated area and wear a face mask and latex or nitrite gloves.*

1 Due to the end-grains of the plywood, a sealer must be used on the inside of the bowl. Put a drop or two of medium CA glue in the bowl and spread it over the piece. Continue to add glue, one or two drops at a time, until the entire inside of the bowl is coated. Spray with activator.

2 Sand lightly with 320-grit sandpaper.

3 With a waste block on a faceplate, refer to lathe manufacturer's

instructions to make a "jam-fit" chuck. Remount the bowl in the lathe securely seated in the jam-fit chuck.

4 Finish shaping the base and turn the bottom of the bowl concave with a small bowl gouge. Sand with the soft-sanding disks.

5 Seal the outside of the bowl in the same manner as the inside. After sanding the bowl with 320-grit sandpaper, spray Deft lacquer on the bowl. ●

TRINKET CATCH-ALL

Design by Loretta Mateik

Inlaid strips of decorative veneer and ball feet add big style to a small project.

PROJECT NOTE

Select paint colors to compliment the inlay strip used.

CUTTING

1 Set the table saw blade angle to 15 degrees; set the fence 1¾ inches from the long point of the cut. Rip the ⅜-inch birch plywood once to make a ⅜x1¾x12-inch piece with one long edge cut at a 15-degree angle. With the straight edge against the fence, rip the plywood again to create a second piece identical to the first. Mark the sides with the long point "inside" and the sides with the short point "outside."

2 With the blade still at 15 degrees, cut the ¼-inch birch plywood so the long-point measurements are 3½x2½ inches for box bottom (Fig 1).

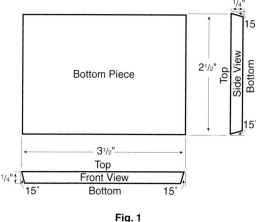

**Fig. 1
Box Bottom**

3 Using the ¼-inch straight bit set to cut a depth matching the thickness of the ¼-inch-wide veneer inlay strip, rout a dado for the inlay down the length of each ⅜-inch plywood piece, with the bottom of the dado ¾-inch from the bottom.

4 Set the angle of the table saw blade to 45 degrees.

Referring to cutting layout on page 108, mark each 12-inch-long piece to cut one front piece and one side piece. *Note: The long point of the angle cuts should be on the outside of each piece.* Line up the first piece with the blade so the cut will follow the mark; slide the miter gauge up to the base of the piece and tighten miter gauge to this angle. Make four of the corner cuts (either all right or all left cuts) from this side, then switch the miter gauge past 90 degrees to the same angle setting and cut the opposite corners (Fig. 2).

5 Dry-fit together using a rubber band in the inlay dado to hold box together. Adjust fit as necessary.

PROJECT SIZE
5x4x2¼ inches

TOOLS
- Table saw with miter gauge
- Router with ¼-inch straight bit
  Compound miter saw (optional)
- Craft knife

SUPPLIES
- ⅜-inch Baltic birch plywood:
  6x12 inches

- ¼-inch Baltic birch plywood:
  4x3 inches
- Veneer inlay strip: ¼x24 inches
- Four ¾-inch wooden balls
- Sandpaper
- Wood glue
- DecoArt Americana acrylic
  paints: lamp black #DA067, slate
  grey #DA068 and antique white
  #DA058
- Matte sealer
- Satin varnish

Disassemble; sand rough edges smooth and wipe clean.

ASSEMBLE & FINISH

1 Seal all surfaces of each piece with matte sealer. Sand lightly; wipe clean.

2 Glue box together; secure with rubber band. Let dry

3 Fill in small spaces and gaps with wood filler; let dry. Sand smooth and wipe clean.

4 Base-coat the inside of box and four wooden balls with *antique white*; base-coat the rest of box with a 4:1 mixture of *slate grey* and *lamp black*. **Note:** *Do not base-coat the inlay dado.*

5 Use the craft knife to cut the inlay strip to fit in the dado on each side of the box; glue in place.

6 Sand a small flat section on the bottom of each of the balls; glue to bottom corners. Let dry.

7 Finish with several light coats of varnish following manufacturer's instructions. ●

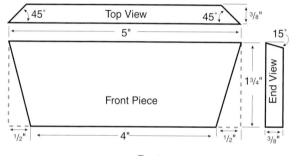

Front

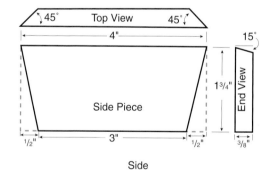

Side

Fig. 2
Box Front/Back and Sides

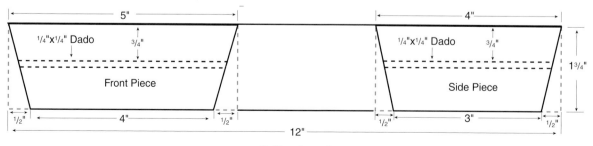

Cutting Layout

PARQUET-TRAY

Design by Annellen and Alex Simpkins

Easy geometric shapes combine in a dynamic design on the plywood base of this serving tray.

MAIN PATTERN

1 Using the patterns provided for square and parallelogram shapes, cut a few of each shape for templates from the 12x12-inch piece of ¼-inch lauan. **Note:** *Cut shapes with craft knife* *using the cutting mat and straightedge.*

2 Trim and refine templates to the exact size and angles needed.

Note: *Make extra pieces of all veneer pieces—some a little larger—for replacements in case of breakage.*

TEMPLATE SYSTEM

1 Butt a straight piece of wood against the veneer, then butt the straightedge against the wood; remove the wood without moving the straightedge. Cut the veneer along the straightedge (Photo 1).

2 Place the lauan template on the veneer. Align the edges using the straight piece of wood (Photo 2), butt the straightedge against the wood, remove the wood and cut veneer against the straightedge. **Note:** *Using the straightedge will prevent marring the edge of the template.* Use this method throughout: Place the template, align with the straight wood, hold and cut with the straightedge.

CUTTING VENEER

1 Beginning with the square shape, use the template to cut six birch veneer squares, one at a time. Maintain the straightedge as a reference.

2 Stack all six squares together. Secure with a piece of wood to prevent any movement. On the shooting board, plane each edge of the veneer stack exactly the same. Check

PROJECT SIZE
18x14x1½ inches

TOOLS
- Craft knife
- Self-healing cutting mat
- Metal straightedge
- Shooting board
- Angle jig
- Low-angle block plane
- Square sanding block
- Table saw with rip blade, crosscut blade and dado set
- Sharp 2-inch chisel
- Eight C-clamps
- Random orbit sander with 220-grit disks
- Japanese dozuki saw*
- Band saw*
- Small files
- Six bar clamps

SUPPLIES
- ¹⁄₄₀-inch or thicker veneers: one 6x36-inch piece birch, one 6x36-inch piece walnut and one 8x36-inch piece mahogany
- ¼-inch lauan: one 14x18-inch sheet (flat and clean with no voids or chips) and one 12x12-inch sheet
- ½-inch mahogany: 2 board feet
- ⅝-inch-wide light-duty masking tape
- Veneer tape
- Titebond veneer glue
- Good quality varnishing brush
- 2x2-inch hardwood**: eight 16-inch lengths (for press bars)
- ¾-inch birch plywood: two 14x18-inch pieces (for press boards)
- Waxed paper
- 400-grit sandpaper
- Salad Bowl Finish food-grade wood finish
- Fine steel wool

* A router with ¼-inch straight bit and template guide may be substituted for the Japanese Dozuki saw and band saw.

** Measurements given are actual, not nominal. Standard nominal lumber will need to be ripped and/or planed to size.

that the squares are all the same size and the corners are exactly 90 degrees.

3 Next, cut seven birch and eight walnut veneer parallelograms. Set the straight piece of wood against the template over the veneer. Keep the veneer and template pressed against the straight piece of wood and chop the end with the 2-inch sharp chisel. The angles must begin and end exactly at the boundaries of the squares. Fine-tune to the exact angles with the block plane or sanding block using the shooting board and angle jig with a stack.

4 When all the squares and parallelograms are cut, carefully tape them together in an esthetically pleasing pattern. A unified pattern is the goal here, so lay out the whole pattern with masking tape first (Photo 3), then go back to do minor trimming and fitting. The shooting board will help keep the project straight during fitting.

5 Once the main pattern is together, trim the four outside edges on the shooting board to prep for the border.

BORDER

1 Cut out the four ¾-inch-wide border strips. Cut two 20-inch and two 16-inch lengths. Perfect the edges with the shooting board. **_Tip:_** _Use a press bar of wood set back about ⅛-inch from the edge to safely hold down the strip._

2 Tape the border pieces onto the tray pattern. Overlap the ends.

3 In pencil, mark a 45-degree angle at the corners of the border. Using the sharp 2-inch chisel, press-cut the top layer of veneer and mark the under layer. Lift away the top piece and chop the under layer ever so slightly longer (about ¹⁄₆₄ inch) to allow for the thickness of the cutting tool. Cut all four corners, then tape border in place.

CORNER PIECES

1 Decide what direction the grain should go for the corner pieces, then trace the two corner shapes on the mahogany veneer. Use the straightedge on the self-healing mat to cut out these shapes slightly larger than the outline. Dry-fit and trim to fit.

2 Examine pattern to see if any light shows through the joints. Trim and refine as necessary.

ASSEMBLE

1 Turn entire pattern over and apply veneer tape. Tape all joints. **_Tip:_** _Use a sponge to lightly moisten the tape. Too much water may cause the veneer to buckle and warp._

2 Crosscut the 8-inch mahogany veneer into two 18-inch lengths and edge-fit them together. Cut the rectangle down to just greater than 14x18 inches. Use the shooting board to make the center joint tight if necessary.

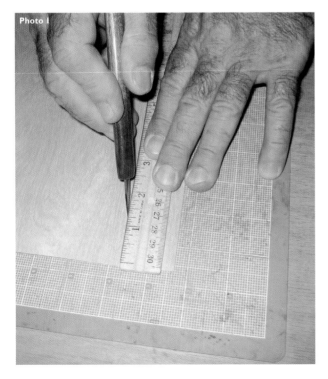

Photo 1

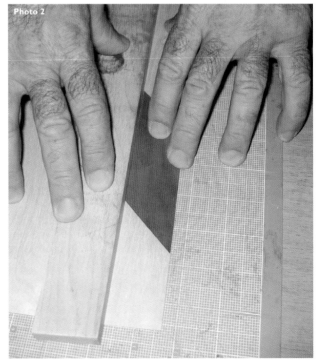

Photo 2

Tape with masking tape, then flip over and tape with the veneer tape.

3 Flatten the unit as it dries by pressing the top parquet veneer and the bottom mahogany veneer into a newspaper sandwich as follows: flat surface, mahogany veneer, newspaper, parquet veneer, flat ¾-inch plywood piece. Let dry for several hours, ideally overnight. Once dry, gently remove masking tape from face of veneers. Remove all of the tape residue cleanly. *Tip: Sometimes a bit of goo-off remover helps remove the masking tape without removing or ripping wood grain as well.*

GLUING

Note: Gather glue, glue brush, press bars, clamps, ¾-inch plywood press plates, masking tape and waxed paper together for efficiency and to stay ahead of setting glue. A second set of hands to help may also be helpful.

1 Apply Titebond veneer glue first to the mahogany bottom veneer piece

on the side with no tape on it. Apply by pouring glue onto the center of the veneer and spreading it quickly and evenly with the varnish brush. Set this piece aside.

2 Spread a light, even coat of glue on the 14x18-inch piece of lauan plywood. Place the two glued surfaces together with edges aligned.

3 Carefully turn the plywood over and apply glue as above, first to the parquet veneer piece, then to the lauan plywood. Place the glued surfaces together, aligning the edges. Secure together with 1-inch strips of masking tape wrapped over each side close to the corners. Inspect the veneered plywood making sure the veneers haven't slipped from the core.

4 Space four press bars on the work surface. Place one ¾-inch plywood press board on top of the press bars, place a layer of waxed paper on top of the board, gently set the veneered

lauan on top of the waxed paper, then cover with another piece of waxed paper, the other ¾-inch press board, and the remaining press bars. Clamp in place with the C-clamps, beginning with the center press bars, then the outer ones, moving the pressure from the inside out (Photo 4). Let dry overnight.

SIDES & HANDLES

1 On the table saw, rip the ½-inch mahogany into four 1½-inch strips. Rip one or two extras for insurance.

2 Cut a ¼x¼-inch dado in the bottom inside edge of each piece, beginning ¾-inch from the bottom.

3 Cut the dadoed sides into two 14-inch and two 18-inch lengths. Find the center of the short side and mark 1½-inches each way. Draw a 45-degree angle from this point and the bottom of the dado, out to the bottom of the side. Cut with the Japanese saw, band saw or a router template.

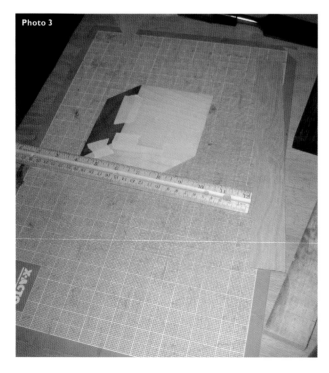

Photo 3

Photo 4

Underside of tray

4 Cut a half-lap into the ends of the short sides to receive the long sides. Cut them deep enough to hide the dado in the short side when the tray is assembled.

FINISH

1 Shape the handle cutouts, handle pieces and side pieces using the small files, random orbit sander and sanding block. Slightly bevel all edges.

2 Using the random orbit sander and 220-grit sandpaper, very gently sand evenly until all the veneer tape has been removed.

3 Fine-sand with 400-grit sandpaper.

4 Pre-oil all the parts with Salad Bowl Finish. Build the surface with several coats.

FINAL ASSEMBLY

1 Apply a thin, even coat of glue to the lap joints and dado joints. Place veneered panel into ¼x¼-inch dado on all sides. Using bar clamps, clamp in four directions at the joints, then place one clamp in the center of each dadoed side, carefully protecting the tray with press bars on all four sides.

2 Pull the dados in snug. Let dry and remove excess glue.

3 If additional flattening of lap joints is needed, do so with a file then reapply the Salad Bowl Finish.

4 Rub the finished tray lightly with fine steel wool; wipe carefully, then apply one final coat of Finish. ●

Parallelogram

Square

SIX-DRAWER CLOCK

Design by Patti J. Ryan

A clock face surrounded by tiny drawers lets you keep track of time and money.

CUTTING

1 From ¼-inch plywood, cut two 3x7-inch pieces for shelves (C); set scraps aside.

2 From ³⁄₁₆ inch oak veneer plywood, cut two 3x8-inch pieces for drawer faces (J), six 2⅜x1⅞-inch pieces for drawer fronts (G), six 2¾x1⅞-inch pieces for drawer backs (D), four 2¹¹⁄₁₆x1⅞-inch pieces for short drawer sides (E) and eight 3¹¹⁄₁₆x1⅞-inch pieces for long drawer sides (F).

3 From ⅛-inch plywood, cut two 2¾x3-inch pieces for short drawer bottoms (H) and four 2¾x4-inch for long drawer bottoms (I).

4 From the ½-inch oak-veneer plywood, cut a 9x30-inch piece. Set the table saw blade to cut a 45-degree angle; cut both 9-inch ends. Move the fence so the next cut will be 9 inches from long point to long point; referring to Fig. 1, make one cut across the board. **Note:** *Long points should be on same side of each board.* Next, flip remaining 21-inch board around so the opposite end is against the fence. Make a cut across the board. This will result in a second 9x9-inch piece. Decide which piece will be the front and the back (A).

5 Flip the remaining piece over so short side face is on the table saw deck. Move the fence so the next cut will be 4 inches from long point to long point. Make the cut. Flip remaining board around so opposite end is against the fence and make the next cut. This will result in the second 4x9-inch piece. Decide which will be the top and bottom (B).

6 Sand all cuts with the 80-grit sanding block to remove rough edges. Wipe clean.

CASE

1 **Note:** *The inside measurements of front and back (A) from short point to short point should be 8 inches. If it is not, adjust the following measurements accordingly.* On both front and back (A), measure and mark 2¹¹⁄₁₆ and 2¹⁵⁄₁₆

PROJECT SIZE

11¾x4x10 inches

TOOLS

- Carpenter's square
- Table saw
- Miter saw
- Sanding block with 80-grit sandpaper
- Drill
- Craft knife
- Nail set
- Bench-style disc sander (optional)

SUPPLIES

- ½-inch oak-veneer plywood: 10x30 inches (grain running with 30-inch length)
- ¼-inch plywood: 8x10 inches
- ³⁄₁₆-inch oak-veneer plywood: 15x20 inches
- ⅛-inch plywood or lauan: 6x12 inches
- Wood glue
- Painter's tape
- Finish nails: ¾- and 1-inch
- Small brad nails
- Stainable wood filler
- 220-grit sandpaper
- Six 1-inch wooden knobs or beads
- Four 1¼-inch wooden ball knobs
- DecoArt Americana water-based stain conditioner #DSA33
- DecoArt Americana water-based light oak stain #AMS08
- DecoArt Americana Satins satin varnish #DSA28
- DecoArt Americana matte spray sealer #DAS13
- Paste wax (optional)
- Desired clock mechanism

inches from the top short-point edge, and 2¹¹⁄₁₆ and 2⁷⁄₁₆ inches from the bottom short-point edge. Place front and back boards side by side with the tops and bottoms flush and use the carpenter's square to draw a line across both boards at all four marks.

Tip: *Apply masking tape to an area prior to drilling the pilot hole. Drill the pilot holes through the tape, set the nail*

heads, and add wood filler. Let dry. Remove tape and sand filler flush.

2 Using a bit the same diameter as the ¾-inch finish nail, predrill two holes from the inside out between each set of lines.

3 On the inside of the front piece, draw an X from corner to corner both ways; use a nail set to mark the

center, then predrill hole for the clock assembly as recommended by the clock manufacturer.

4 On the outside of the bottom piece (B), measure 1 inch from each end at each corner. Drill a pilot hole from the outside in at each of these four marks for attaching ball knobs. On the inside, drill a countersink for the screw heads.

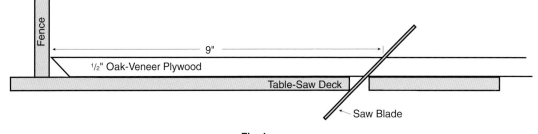

Fig. 1
Case Miters

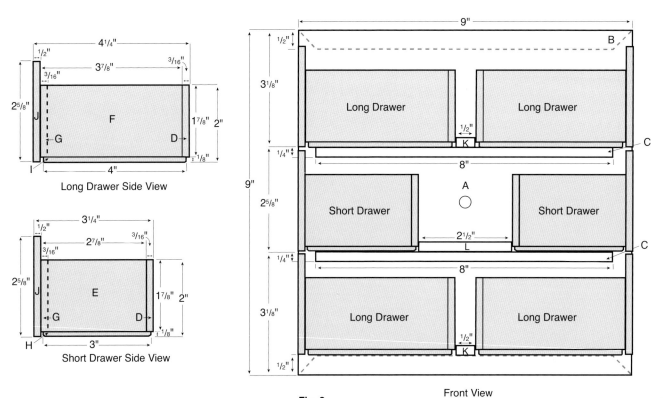

Long Drawer Side View

Short Drawer Side View

Front View

Fig. 2
Cross-Section Assembly Diagrams

5 Dry-fit the front, back, top and bottom together and tape with two or three strips across each joint. Drill three pilot holes through each side of the top (B) and each side of the bottom (B) so the finish nails can be driven into the front and back (A).

6 Lift the tape from one corner and lay the entire box out flat. Apply wood glue to the miters following manufacturer's instructions. Tape the box back together again and secure with 1-inch finish nails through the top and bottom (B) and into the mitered ends of the sides. Remove tape and wipe off any excess glue with a damp rag.

7 Insert ¾-inch screws through bottom from the inside; screw on 1¼-inch wooden ball knobs for feet.

8 Referring to Fig. 2, slide shelves (C) in place ½ inch in from each end; temporarily tape in place, if necessary. Glue the edges, then secure with ¾-inch finish nails.

9 Fill nail and screw holes, as well as voids in the ends of the plywood box with wood filler. Let dry, then sand smooth.

DRAWER BOX

1 Sand drawer pieces (D, E, F, G, H and I) with the sanding block, slightly beveling the bottom perimeter of the six drawers.

2 Assemble all six drawer boxes by butting the sides (E, F) into the back (D), then front (G) into the sides. Secure with glue and brad nails. Center the bottoms (H, I) and glue in place.

3 Set the drawer boxes out in pairs: two long, two short and two and long. Measure from the inside top of the case to the top of the first shelf (2¹¹⁄₁₆ inches on model project). Use that measurement to mark and cut the top drawer face of each side, measuring also from the top. Set this piece with the drawer to which it will be attached. ***Note: For fluidity of grain pattern, mark and cut all three faces for the right drawers from one board (J) and for all three left drawers from the other board (J).***

4 Measure from the inside bottom of the case to the top of the bottom shelf and cut the bottom drawer face to this measurement (2¹¹⁄₁₆ inches on model project), measuring also from the bottom of the face boards. The remaining piece will be the middle drawer face. Set these pieces with the drawers to which they will be attached.

5 Glue each drawer face onto each drawer, centered left to right and flush with the bottom.

6 Mark the center of each drawer face and drill a pilot hole for the #6 wood screw through the front to the inside. Attach 1-inch wooden balls from the inside with ¾-inch screws.

7 Fit the drawers into their respective slots. If spacing needs to be adjusted, tape or glue a piece of veneer to the bottom of the drawer needing the adjustment. Using a permanent marker, indicate the location of each drawer on

SIX-DRAWER CLOCK CUTTING CHART
(Actual Sizes)

P	T	W	L	#
A	½"	9"	9"	2
B	½"	4"	9"	2
C	¼"	3"	8"	2
D	³⁄₁₆"	2¾"	1⅞"	6
E	³⁄₁₆"	2¹¹⁄₁₆"	1⅞"	4
F	³⁄₁₆"	3¹¹⁄₁₆"	1⅞"	8
G	³⁄₁₆"	2¾"	1⅞"	6
H	⅛"	2¾"	2⅞"	2
I	⅛"	2¾"	3⅞"	4
J	³⁄₁₆"	3"	2¹¹⁄₁₆"	6
K	¼"	¼"	3"	2
L	¼"	2¼"	3"	1

the back of its face (i.e. L-top, R-top, etc.). Remove drawers.

8 Insert clock shaft through the hole from inside the case. Add extra washers on the inside if necessary to adjust the length of the threaded post to the front of the box. Secure with the washer and locking ring on the front as instructed in the manufacturer's instructions. Tape the post to protect it during the finishing process.

9 Slide one drawer into place and hold it flush with the sides of the box; mark the back of the box on the shelf. Remove drawer and repeat with each remaining drawer. From scraps of ¼-inch plywood, cut two short drawer stops (K) to fit between long drawers (¼ inch) and one long drawer stop (L) to fit between short drawers (2¼ inches). Glue the stops in place on tops of shelves; let dry.

FINISH

1 On case front, mark the center of each edge (4½ inches). Lightly draw a line connecting the center marks to form a diamond shape on the front. Draw parallel lines ⅛ inch inside the first lines. Divide each side of the diamond into three equal sections, each approximately 2⅛ inches. Draw a checkerboard pattern by connecting each mark to the corresponding mark on the opposite side of the diamond (Fig. 3). Using the metal straight edge and craft knife, score penciled lines.

2 Apply stain conditioner to all wood surfaces. Lightly sand with 220-grit sandpaper; remove dust.

3 Use painter's tape to mask off five of the nine squares and the area outside the diamond shape. With a foam brush, apply *light oak* stain. Let set five to 10 minutes, then wipe off. Let dry 30 minutes. Repeat with second coat. Remove masking tape. **Note:** *Use a cotton swab to wipe off stain that may have seeped under the edges of the tape.*

4 Mask-off the checkerboard design, leaving the diamond border exposed. Stain the front, sides, back and inside of the case with *light oak,* letting set and wiping off as done previously. Let final coat dry 30 minutes, then remove tape.

5 Apply stain conditioner to all surfaces of the drawers, then stain; let dry.

6 Apply satin varnish to all surfaces, following manufacturer's instructions. Spray with several light coats of matte finish, letting dry after each coat. If desired, apply a coat of paste wax; let dry 5 minutes, then buff with a soft cloth.

7 Assemble face of clock insert following manufacturer's instructions, then insert drawers in their proper locations. ●

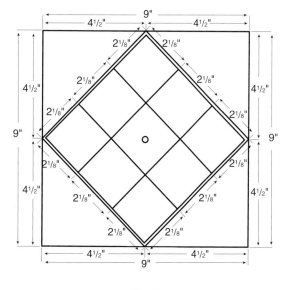

Fig. 3
Diamond Pattern

WIGGLE-BOARD CLOCK

Design by Patti J. Ryan

Bendable plywood, or wiggle board, is easy to bend around gently curving shapes.

CUTTING

1 Set the table saw to rip an 8-inch width and make two passes with ¼-inch plywood so there are two 8x12-inch pieces for the front and back. Reset the table-saw fence and rip a 2x12-inch strip; cut this to 8 inches for the bottom plate.

PROJECT SIZE
8¾x3¼x13 inches

TOOLS
- Table saw
- Carpenter's square
- Utility knife
- Compass
- Jigsaw or band saw
- Bench disk sander
- Miter saw
- Clamps
- Nail set

SUPPLIES
- ¼-inch paintable plywood: 12x24 inches
- ½x1¼-inch pine or poplar*: 24 inches
- ⅛-inch lauan or plywood: 12x24 inches
- ⅛-inch bendable plywood: 6x38 inches

- 3¼x3¼-inch solid wood appliqué
- ⅜x1⅜-inch colonial doorstop molding: 30 inches
- Wood glue
- Nails: ⅝-inch brad and ¾-inch finish
- 2¹⁵⁄₁₆-inch-bezel gold clock movement
- DecoArt Americana Satins Primer & Stain Blocker #DSA34, rustic red #DSA42 and satin varnish #DSA28
- DecoArt Americana Dazzling Metallics: glorious gold #DA071
- DecoArt Weathered Wood crackling medium #DAS8
- DecoArt Americana Gloss Spray Sealer #DAS12

* Measurements given are actual, not nominal. Standard nominal lumber will need to be ripped and/or planed to size.

2 From the ⅛-inch lauan, cut one 7x11-inch piece for the first overlay, and one 6x10-inch piece for second overlay using the carpenter's square as a straightedge, and a utility knife.

3 Cut seven 2-inch spacers from the ½x1¼-inch flat stock.

4 On the ¼-inch front piece, measure and mark 4 inches from the top and 4 inches from the side at the same point (Fig. 1). Using this cross-mark for the pivot point of the compass, set the compass to draw a 4-inch-diameter circle, then draw the top arc across the top. Stack the front and back pieces together and cut both arcs at the same time with the jigsaw or band saw.

5 In the same manner as in the previous step, mark arcs on the ⅛-inch lauan pieces, making a 3½-inch-diameter circle for the 7x11-inch first overlay and a 3-inch-diameter circle as the measurement for the 6x10-inch second overlay. Cut both arcs with the jigsaw or band saw. Using the sanding block or disk sander, round over the front edges of both overlays.

6 Sand the cut edges of all pieces smooth with the sanding pad or disk sander. Wipe clean.

7 Follow manufacturer's instructions to determine the size of the hole for the clock. Using the center mark for the

arc on each piece, draw the appropriate size hole with a compass and use the jigsaw to cut that size in both ⅛-inch overlays and the front. Sand cut edges. Remove dust with tack cloth.

8 Glue the overlays to the front, making sure the clock holes are aligned.

ASSEMBLE

1 Place the bottom plate between the front and back pieces, flush with the outside edges and the bottom, and glue and nail in place with brads.

2 Referring to the assembly diagram, mark the positions of the seven spacers at the vertical center of the front and back pieces, on each side centered 4 inches from the top and bottom and on each side centered at the middle of the arc. Attach spacers as shown in diagram, beginning at the top and working down.

3 Using a utility knife and carpenter's square, cut a piece of ⅛-inch bendable plywood 2½ inches (the width of the clock case from front to back) by 38 inches. Beginning at the center top and working down each side, glue and brad nail the wiggle board in place along the front and back plywood pieces and into the spacers. End by gluing and nailing into the bottom plate.

4 Trim off excess with the utility knife then sand edges flush with the clock front and back.

5 Cut the colonial doorstop molding with mitered corners to fit around the bottom of the clock case. With top of molding flush with bottom of first overlay, glue and nail to clock case with ¾-inch finish nails. Secure the miters with brads.

6 Set nails with the nail set and fill all holes and gaps with paintable wood filler; let dry. Sand flush and remove dust.

7 Glue appliqué to face overlay below clock opening. Clamp and let set until dry.

FINISHING

1 Apply primer; let dry 30 minutes, then sand lightly with 220-grit wet/dry sandpaper. Wipe clean and let dry.

2 Apply two base coats of glorious gold, letting dry 30 minutes between coats.

3 Following manufacturer's instructions, apply crackle finish. When tacky, apply generous stokes of rustic red. Set aside overnight to dry completely.

4 If necessary, lightly sand any uneven paint with 220-grit wet/dry sandpaper. Gently wipe clean. Lightly

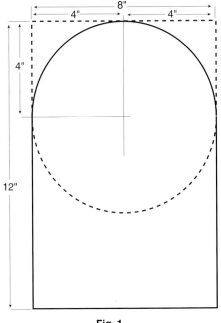

Fig. 1
Front Arc

dry-brush gold over molding edges and top surface of appliqué. Let dry.

5 Apply one or two coats of satin varnish, following manufacturer's instructions, then add several coats of spray gloss sealer.

6 Insert batteries in clock and set time. Press clock in place and align clock face. ●

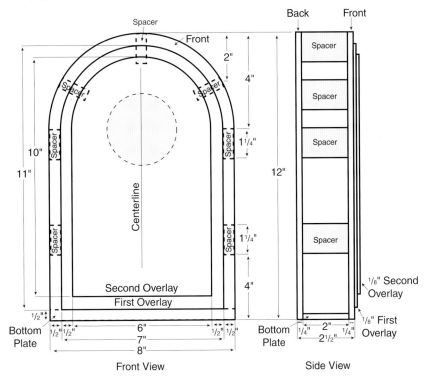

Assembly Diagram

RAINBOW RING HOLDER

Design by Linda Van Gehuchten

Colorful dyed plywood, turned to perfection, makes an eye-catching statement.

Photo 1

PROJECT SIZE

Approximately 2 inches in diameter x 5 inches tall

TOOLS

- Band saw
- Drill or drill press with ½-inch Forstner bit
- Calipers
- Lathe
- Turning tools: skew (optional), roughing out gouge, spindle gouge, ¼-inch bowl gouge and parting tool
- Cordless drill with sanding disks

SUPPLIES

- Colorwood dyed plywood: one 2x2x2-inch block
- ½-inch wooden dowel: 1½ inches
- 1x1-inch ebony or other dark wood*: 3 inches
- Cyanoacrylate (CA) glue and aerosol activator
- Latex gloves
- Deft spray lacquer

* Measurements given are actual, not nominal. Standard nominal lumber will need to be ripped and/or planed to size.

PREPARE COLORWOOD

1 Glue Colorwood block to a waste block on the faceplate, or prepare the waste block to be held in the chuck (Photo 1).

2 On the lathe, find the center of the waste block and make an indentation with the skew for the drill bit.

3 Using the ½-inch Forstner bit, drill the hole in the block of Colorwood on the lathe 1-inch deep.

TURNING
Base

1 Bring up the tailstock to support the Colorwood block.

2 Rough-cut the Colorwood block into a cylinder with a roughing out gouge (Photo 2).

Photo 2

Photo 3

Photo 4

3 Shape the base with a spindle gouge.

4 Smooth out with sanding disks beginning at 80-grit and progressing to 220-grit.

5 Apply CA glue, adding one drop at a time and spreading it out until surface is covered; mist with the activator. ***Caution:*** *Work in a well-ventilated area and wear a face mask and latex or nitrile gloves.* Sand with 320-grit sandpaper.

6 With the parting tool, part off the base of the ring holder at the waste block.

7 Reverse chuck the ring holder by drilling a ½-inch hole ¾ inch deep in the waste block, gluing the ½-inch dowel into it then attaching the ring holder (Photos 3 and 4). ***Note:*** *This will allow for the finishing of the bottom of the ring holder.*

8 With the ¼-inch bowl gouge, cut the foot concave. Sand and seal with the CA glue as above.

Stem

1 Find the centers of the ends of the ebony and rough out between the centers. Turn one end down to ½ inch by ¾ inch long for a post. Check with the calipers. Dry-fit stem into base.

2 Make another jig using a waste block with a ½-inch hole in its center. Insert the stem into this waste block. Bring up the tailstock to support the other end of the stem, and mark ½ inch from the tailstock. Shape and sand the stem.

3 Part off or cut off the ½-inch waste on the tailstock end.

4 Remove the stem from the waste block. Apply a drop of CA glue in the hole of the base, then spray activator on the tenon of the stem and twist into place so the stem is well-seated.

5 Finish with a light coat of Deft spray lacquer. ●

SIMPLY PLYWOOD RING HOLDER

Design by Linda Van Gehuchten

The simple beauty of birch plywood is on display in this handy sink-side gadget.

BASE

1 Using wood glue, glue and clamp the three 3x20-inch strips together making one 2¼x3x20-inch block. Let dry for two hours.

2 With the belt sander, clean the dried glue from one long edge of the block. Rip this block to 2¾ inches wide.

3 Cut the end of the blank at a 45-degree angle. Referring to Fig. 1, cut two pieces each 2½ inches long with the ends of each running parallel.

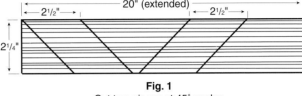

Fig. 1
Cut two pieces at 45° angles
with ends of each piece parallel.

4 Using the wood glue, glue the cut edges of these two pieces together to make a V shape, like a chevron (Fig. 2), with the points meeting perfectly. Immediately clean up any glue squeeze-out on the inside and outside with a damp rag. Let dry for two hours.

5 Cut the bottom of the chevron at a 45-degree angle 1⅝ inch from the bottom point (Fig. 3). This flat surface will be the ring holder bottom.

Fig. 2
Glue cut edges together
to form a chevron with
grain running as shown.

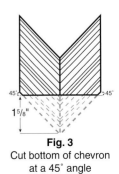

Fig. 3
Cut bottom of chevron
at a 45° angle
1⅝" from the bottom.

PROJECT SIZE

Approximately 2¾ inches in diameter x 4 inches tall

TOOLS

- Clamps
- Belt sander or jointer
- Miter saw
- Band saw
- Combination square
- Lathe
- Turning tools: rough-out gouge, spindle gouge bowl gouge and parting tool
- Cordless drill with 80- through 320-grit sanding disks

SUPPLIES

- ¾-inch Baltic birch plywood: three 3x20-inch strips
- ¾x1-inch walnut*: 4½ inches
- Titebond Original wood glue
- Cyanoacrylate (CA) glue and aerosol activator
- Latex gloves
- Sandpaper
- Deft spray lacquer

* Measurements given are actual, not nominal. Standard nominal lumber will need to be ripped and/or planed to size.

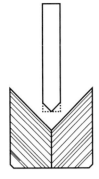

Fig. 4
Cut a point on the ³/₄" edge
of the walnut stem.

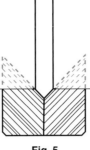

Fig. 5
Cut off points of chevron
using band saw.

6 Referring to Fig. 4, cut a point on the ¾-inch end of the walnut stem using 45-degree angles. Check the fit into the inside V of the chevron. Adjust as needed for a tight fit then glue the stem into the plywood base using wood glue. Let dry 2 hours.

7 On the band saw, cut off the pointed ends of the plywood chevron even with the base of the stem (Fig. 5).

8 Put a waste block on the faceplate and mark the center while it is turning on the lathe. True up the face so it is flat. Draw a straight line through the center to both ends of the waste block. Glue the chevron onto the waste block, lining up the centerline (chevron glue line) and center points. **Note:** *Matching centers is critical to the outcome of this project.*

TURNING

1 Mount the faceplate and blank on the lathe. Bring up the tailstock to the walnut stem and secure. Set the lathe speed to 800 rpm.

2 Round off the plywood turning blank to a cylinder with the rough-out gouge, then shape with the spindle and bowl gouges.

3 On the stem, mark off ½ inch from the tailstock live center. Use a bowl gouge to transit from the plywood base to rounding off the base of the stem.

4 Shape the stem with a rough-out gouge first, then refine with the spindle gouge. The stem should not be more than ½ inch in diameter for the rings to fit.

5 Sand with a sanding disk on a cordless drill. Begin with 80-grit and sand progressively up to 320-grit.

FINISH

1 With the piece still on the lathe, but the lathe turned off, put a drop of CA glue on the plywood and spread it out. **Caution:** *Work in a well-ventilated area and wear a face mask and latex or nitrite gloves.* Keep adding and spreading the glue one drop at a time until the entire piece is coated, then spray with the activator to harden. Buff with 320-grit sandpaper.

2 Part-off the ring holder from the waste block.

3 Drill a ½-inch hole in the waste block, wrap the stem in thin packing and slide the waste block over the stem. Re-chuck the waste block and bring up the tailstock just enough to hold the ring holder in place.

4 Make a light concave cut on the bottom with a sharp bowl gouge.

5 Remove the ring holder from the waste block. Hand-sand any imperfections and spray with Deft lacquer. ●

PORTABLE BOX MIRROR

Design by Barbara Greve

Fill the box with silk flowers for an elegant accent to any room.

CUTTING

Note: Refer to plywood cutting chart.

1 Use the table saw to rip one 3½-inch-wide piece of red oak plywood; cut two 8-inch lengths from this width (box front and back) and two 2½-inch lengths (box sides).

2 Rip another piece of red oak plywood 8 inches wide; cut the length of this piece 17 inches (mirror back).

3 From the remaining plywood sheet, cut a 2½-inch-wide by 7-inch-long piece (bottom).

4 Sand out rough spots on all pieces with 120-grit sandpaper; remove dust.

5 Cut two 8-inch lengths of decorative molding.

ASSEMBLE & FINISH

Note: Use wood glue unless otherwise stated.

1 Iron on veneer edging tape to all four edges of box front and back, all four edges of mirror back and the top and bottom edges of each side piece. Trim off excess veneer with edge trimmer as instructed by manufacturer.

2 Glue box together, butting sides into the box front and back pieces and attaching bottom inside and flush with the bottom edges. Clamp in place; let dry.

3 Attach mirror back by applying glue to the bottom 3½-inches and pressing onto box back with bottom edges flush; secure with 1-inch pockethole screws through mirror back into bottom. Let dry.

4 Glue first piece of decorative molding to mirror back flush at the top; glue second piece to mirror back at the top of box back. Clamp in place; let dry.

5 Fill screw holes with wood filler; let dry then sand smooth. Sand entire unit smooth with 320-grit sandpaper; remove dust.

PROJECT SIZE
8x4x17 inches

TOOLS
- Table saw
- 10-inch compound miter saw
- Household iron with cotton setting
- Edge trimmer
- Wood clamps: two 4-inch and two 15-inch
- 3-inch pockethole system with #2 square driver bit and two #8x1-inch screws
- ¾-inch variable speed drill

SUPPLIES
- ½-inch red oak plywood: 24x24 inches
- ¾-inch red oak iron on veneer: 9 feet
- 5⁄16x¾-inch decorative molding: 2 feet
- 8x12-inch beveled-edge mirror
- Wood glue
- Wood filler
- Glass adhesive
- Sandpaper: 120- and 320-grit
- Four pieces scrap wood
- Mahogany stain
- Satin varnish
- Sawtooth hanger

6 Brush mahogany stain over the entire piece and wipe off excess with paper towel; let dry and sand lightly with 320-grit sandpaper. Repeat process until desired effect is achieved. **Note:** *Keep damp paper towels on hand in case more stain needs to be removed.* Let dry.

7 Apply a coat of varnish following manufacturer's instructions; let dry.

8 Using glass adhesive, glue mirror onto mirror back . Let dry.

9 Attach sawtooth hanger to center back, 1 inch below the top. ●

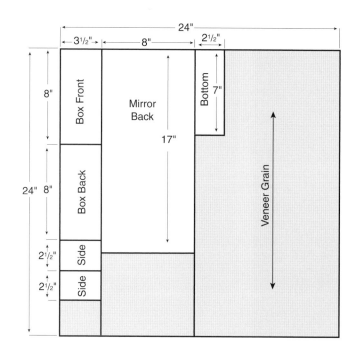

Plywood Cutting Chart

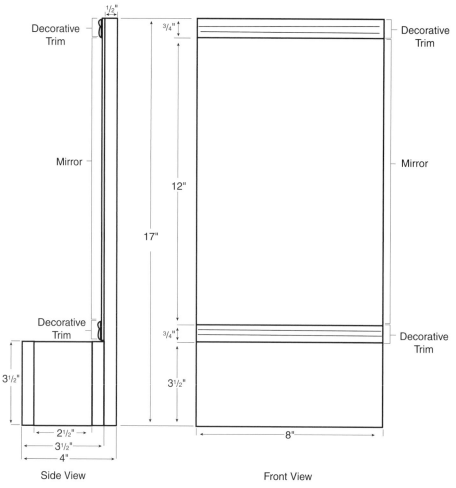

Side View   Front View

Assembly Diagram

SCROLLS & SWIRLS DESK SET

Design by Barbara Greve

Stenciled accents and mini beaded molding add sophistication to a home office.

Desk organizer

CUTTING

1 From the ⅜-inch plywood, cut two 7x11-inch pieces for sides, one 6⅝x10½-inch piece for back divider, one 4⅞x10½-inch piece for front divider, one 7x10¼-inch piece for back, one 3½x10¼-inch piece for front and one 10¼x10¼-inch piece for bottom.

PROJECT SIZE
Organizer: 11¼x11¼x7¼
Frame: 5½x½x6, excluding stand

TOOLS
- Jigsaw
- Router with edge guide and ⅜-inch straight bit
- ⅜-inch variable-speed drill with 5/64- and 5/16-inch bits
- Clamps
- 16-inch scroll saw
- 10-inch drill press with ⅜-inch bit
- Easy Cutter Ultimate wood snips (optional)
- Sander with 80-and 120-grit sandpaper

SUPPLIES
- ⅜-inch plywood: 12 x 48 inches
- ½-inch plywood: 6 x 5½ inch scrap
- ¼-inch plywood: 6 x 5½ inch scrap
- ⅛x3/32-inch beaded trim molding: four 36-inch lengths
- Wood glue
- Wood filler
- 320-grit sandpaper
- Four #6x¾-inch wood screws
- ⅜-inch wooden dowel: one 3-inch length
- Background scroll stencil
- DecoArt Americana Satins acrylic paints: colonial blue #DSA18, bright blue #DSA17 and soft white #DSA02
- DecoArt Staining/Antiquing medium
- DecoArt Americana satin varnish #DSA28

Note: *Refer to Fig. 1 throughout.*

2 Using the ⅜-inch straight bit, rout a 3/16-inch deep dado across the 7-inch width of each side, beginning 3⅝ inches from the front. Rout a second dado in the same manner beginning 7¼-inches from the front.

3 On the outside of one of the side pieces, measure and mark 3¾ inches from the top back edge of the side toward the front, and 3½ inches from the bottom front edge of the side up. Connect these two marks. Using clamps or double-sided tape, secure the two sides together so the dadoes are facing in; cut off the triangle formed by this line, cutting both pieces at the same time.

4 Sand rough places smooth and remove dust.

ASSEMBLE & FINISH

1 Apply glue to one end of the 4⅞- and 6⅝-inch dividers; press into the corresponding side dadoes. **Note:** *Dividers should be ⅜ inch short of bottom edge, and just below top edge of side.* Apply glue to the opposite ends of dividers and both ends of the 3½-inch front and the 7-inch back pieces; assemble box/divider unit. Clamp together loosely.

2 Apply glue to the bottom edges of dividers and on the outside edges of the 10¼x10¼-inch bottom piece; slip bottom in place inside front, back and sides so it is flush with bottom edges. Tighten clamps to hold all together securely. Let dry.

3 Predrill ⁵⁄₆₄-inch holes through sides for two screws into each end of front and back pieces. Drill with ⁵⁄₁₆-inch bit for countersink. Drive in ¾-inch wood screws.

4 Using photo as a guide, cut and glue the beaded trim molding over top edges and around bottom perimeter. Let dry.

5 Fill gaps and screw holes with wood filler. Let dry, then sand smooth.

6 Apply two coats of *soft white* to all surfaces, allowing to dry and sanding with 320-grit sandpaper between coats.

7 Apply scroll stencil using a mixture of one part *bright blue* and three parts *colonial blue*. **Note:** Rub stencil brush out on paper towel to remove excess paint before applying to stencil.

8 Mix the remainder of the paint mixture with an equal amount of gel staining medium. Apply to beaded trim molding with a brush, then wipe off excess. Repeat until desired affect is achieved. Let dry.

9 Apply one or two light coats of varnish following manufacturer's instructions.

Frame
CUTTING

1 For frame front, trace oval template onto ½-inch plywood, centered side to side and 1 inch from the top. Cut out oval with scroll saw; discard oval.

2 For frame back, mark ¼-inch-plywood rectangle ⅞-inch in from the outside edge all the way around; cut out center with scroll saw and discard.

3 Sand rough edges and remove dust.

ASSEMBLE & FINISH

1 Glue frame back and front together with outside edges flush; clamp until dry.

2 Using the drill press and a ⅜-inch bit, drill a ½-inch-deep hole centered side to side on the back of the frame, ½ inch from the bottom.

3 Cut the beaded molding to fit around the face perimeter of the frame; glue in place. Let dry.

4 Finish in same manner as organizer, steps 5–9 of Assemble and Finish.

5 Cut a piece of cardboard to fit into the rectangle

on the frame back; trim photo same size. Insert photo in frame, then back with cardboard; tape edges to secure.

6 For stand, insert ⅜-inch dowel into hole in frame back. ●

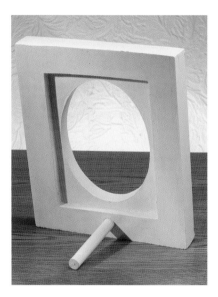

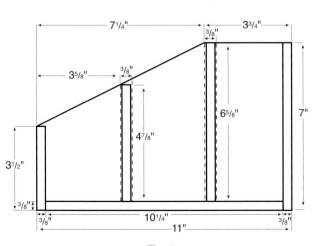

Fig. 1

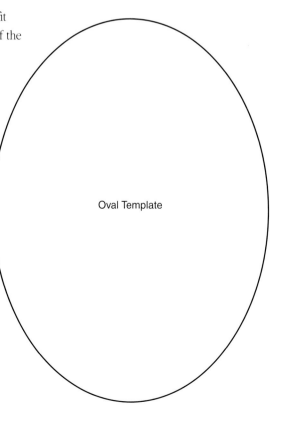

Oval Template

STAIRSTEP DISPLAY LEDGE

Design by Sue Reeves

Exposed plies make a definite design statement in this dramatic display shelf.

INSTRUCTIONS

1 Rip and cut the following from the ¾-inch oak plywood: one 5x18-inch piece for layer 1, one 4¼x16½-inch length for layer 2, one 3½x15-inch piece for layer 3 and one 2¾x13½-inch piece for layer 4.

2 On the bottom of each piece, lightly mark the outline of the next size smaller, centered side to side and flush at the back.

3 Following manufacturer's instructions, use cyanoacrylate glue to adhere layers 1 and 2 together, with layer 2 positioned in the pencil line. Repeat the process to adhere layers 3 and 4 together. Let dry.

4 Glue together both glued sections so layer 3 is inside the lines on the bottom of layer 2. Let dry.

5 Sand all surfaces with 80-, then 120-grit sandpaper until smooth. Remove dust.

6 Spray with two light coats of polyurethane; let dry. Sand lightly then apply a third coat; let dry.

7 Mount hanging hardware to top back edge of layer 1. ●

PROJECT SIZE
18x5x3 inches

TOOLS

- Table saw, or circular saw with edge guide
- Sanding block with 80- and 120-grit sandpaper

SUPPLIES

- ¾-inch oak plywood: 18x18 inches
- Cyanoacrylate (CA) glue
- Gloss spray polyurethane
- Hanging hardware

VERSATILE DISPLAY SHELF

Design by Patti J. Ryan

Make one or a set! Hang this simple reversible shelf to suit your display needs.

CUTTING

1 From ½-inch birch plywood, use the table saw to cut three 3½x24-inch strips.

2 Set the miter saw to cut 45-degree miters. Referring to Fig. 1, cut 3½-inch-wide strips as follows: one 15½-inch length for top; two 11½-inch lengths for sides, three 5½-inch lengths for short horizontals and two 5½-inch lengths for short verticals. **Note:** *Measurements are long point to long point.*

PROJECT SIZE
15½x3½x11½ inches

TOOLS
- Carpenter's square
- Table saw
- Miter saw
- Sanding block with 80-grit sandpaper
- Drill with ¹⁄₁₆-inch bit
- Nail set

SUPPLIES
- ½-inch birch plywood: 12x24 inches
- ⅛-inch plywood or lauan: 12x18 inches

3 Sand smooth with 80-grit sanding block; wipe clean.

ASSEMBLE & FINISH

1 Referring to assembly diagram, dry-fit two short verticals and one short horizontal together to form the small center section, then dry-fit the rest of the shelf frame together. Disassemble and adjust fit if needed.

2 Drill one or two off-setting pilot holes in each side of each corner.

- Wood glue
- Masking tape
- 1-inch finish nails
- Flat-head tacks
- Wood filler
- 220-grit sandpaper
- DecoArt Americana Satins primer and stain blocker #DSA34
- DecoArt Americana Satins soft natural #DSA40 and French blue #DSA43
- DecoArt Americana Satins gloss varnish #DSA27 (optional)
- Sawtooth hanger

3 Beginning with the first small section as before, reassemble the shelf frame by spreading glue on the miters, holding corners together with masking tape and securing with 1-inch finish nails. Glue, tape and finish-nail all other corners, completing the entire frame. Check to make sure the shelf unit is square, then remove tape from all corners and wipe off any excess glue. Let dry.

4 Lay the ⅛-inch plywood on the work surface. Align the top and right sides of the shelf frame just under flush to the top and right edges of the plywood. Outline the left, bottom, and center sections on the plywood. Cut to the inside of the line so the plywood back is slightly smaller than the frame. Turn shelf frame face down and nail the back in place with flat-head tacks.

5 Set the finish nails with the nail set; fill all nail holes and any voids in the plywood edges with wood filler; let dry. Sand surfaces smooth and slightly round over the corners and edges with the 80-grit sanding block; remove dust.

6 Apply a coat of primer/stain blocker to all surfaces; let dry 30 minutes, then sand lightly with 220-grit sandpaper. Wipe clean.

7 Apply two coats of *soft natural* to shelves and back, letting dry after each coat. Paint front edges *French blue* in same manner.

8 If desired, apply a coat of gloss varnish, following manufacturer's instructions.

9 Install hanging hardware on back. ●

15½"

Top
Cut 1.

11½"

Long Side
Cut 2.

5½"

Short Vertical
Cut 2.

5½"

Short Horizontal
Cut 3.

Fig. 1
Miter Cut Layout

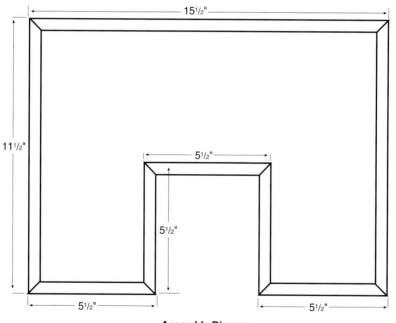

15½"

11½"

5½"

5½"

5½"

5½"

Assembly Diagram

CATTAIL SHADOWS

Design by Delores F. Ruzicka

A mirror accented with the stunning silhouettes of a leaping fish and a stand of cattails bring the cottage look to your home.

INSTRUCTIONS

1 From ¼-inch plywood, cut a 12x15-inch rectangle for the frame. Lightly draw a border 3 inches from each edge; drill a starter hole and cut out the center of the frame using the scroll saw.

2 Join left and right cattail patterns to make a full-size pattern. Transfer cattail and fish patterns to the to remaining plywood and cut with a scroll saw.

3 Drill a hole in each top corner of the frame for the hanging wire.

4 Sand all pieces smooth and remove dust.

5 Apply *black satin* paint to the fish and cattails, making sure that even the crevices are covered. Let dry, then apply a second coat.

6 Apply chestnut stain to frame; let dry. Seal the frame with satin varnish.

7 Glue mirror tile to back of frame; let dry. Using photo as a guide, glue the cattails and fish in place on the front of the frame.

8 Coil the 24-inch length of wire around a pencil. Insert ends of wire from back through holes in frame, and twist to secure. Tie raffia onto the wire. ●

PROJECT SIZE
13¼x¾x15⅞ inches

TOOLS
- Drill with ⅛-inch bit
- Scroll saw
- Palm sander

SUPPLIES
- ¼-inch birch plywood: 15x30 inches (with grain in 15-inch direction), or one 12x15-inch and one 13x16-inch piece
- Sandpaper
- DecoArt Americana Water-Based Stain: chestnut #AMS03
- DecoArt Americana Satins acrylic paint: black satin #DSA25
- DecoArt Americana Satins satin varnish #DSA28
- Wood glue
- 12x12-inch mirror tile
- 20-gauge wire: 24 inches
- Raffia

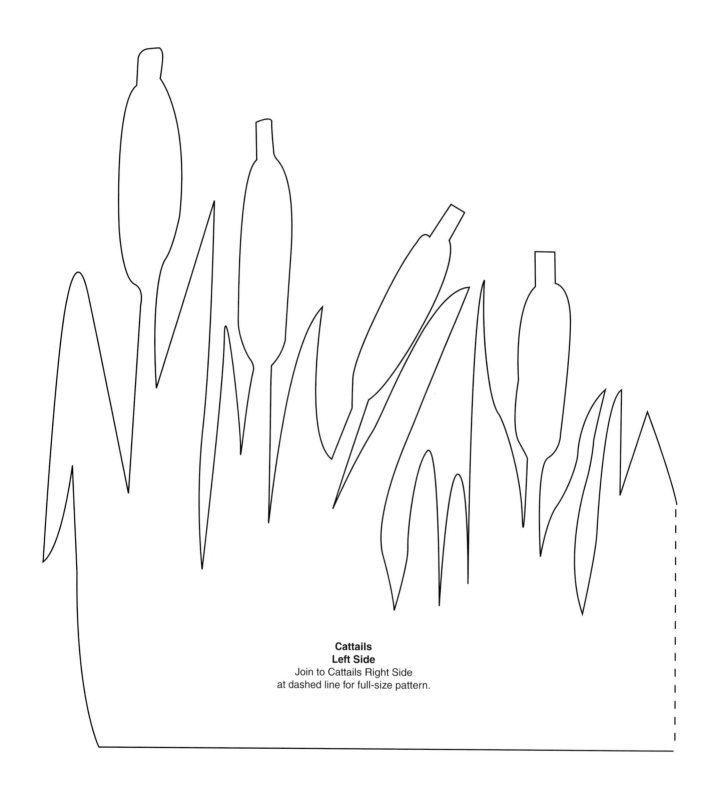

Cattails
Left Side
Join to Cattails Right Side
at dashed line for full-size pattern.

Cattails
Right Side
Join to Cattails Left Side
at dashed line for full-size pattern.

Fish

MEMORIES COLLAGE

Design by Barbara Greve

Display favorite photos in a scrapbook layout for your wall!

PROJECT NOTE

Each frame has eight pieces: four frame face pieces, three center pieces and a back. Throughout instructions, abbreviations are used to indicate each frame as follows: TR (top right), TL (top left), C (center); and BL (bottom left). Label and stack components for each frame together as they are cut.

CUTTING

Note: Use wood snips to cut frame face and center pieces. Use scroll saw to cut back pieces and spacers. Sand cut edges smooth using 120-grit sandpaper; remove dust before finishing.

Frame face pieces

1 From 1⁄8x3⁄8-inch basswood, cut two 33⁄8-inch lengths (TR top/bottom), two 21⁄8-inch lengths (TR sides), two 31⁄4-inch lengths (TL top/bottom) and two 21⁄2-inch lengths (TL sides).

2 From 1⁄16x1⁄2-inch basswood, cut two 5-inch lengths (C top/bottom), two 43⁄4-inch lengths (C sides), two 47⁄8-inch lengths (BL sides) and two 31⁄2-inch lengths (BL top/bottom).

Frame center pieces

1 From 1⁄16x1⁄8-inch basswood, cut two 23⁄4-inch lengths (TR sides), one 35⁄16-inch length (TR bottom), two 33⁄16-inch lengths (TL sides) and one 213⁄16-inch length (TL bottom).

2 From the 1⁄16x1⁄4-inch basswood, cut two 55⁄8-inch lengths (C sides), one 41⁄4-inch length (C bottom), two 41⁄4-inch lengths (BL top/bottom) and one 47⁄8-inch length (BL side).

Frame back pieces & spacers

1 From 1⁄8-inch craft plywood, cut one 27⁄8x33⁄4-inch piece (TR back), one 31⁄4x31⁄4-inch piece (TL back), one 5x53⁄4-inch piece (C back) and one 41⁄2x413⁄16-inch piece (BL back).

2 From 1⁄4x1-inch basswood, cut seven 1-inch lengths for spacers.

3 From 1⁄8x1-inch basswood, cut five 1-inch lengths for spacers.

ASSEMBLE & FINISH

Note: Use wood glue throughout unless otherwise stated.

1 Glue the TR, TL, and C frame faces together by butting side pieces into top and bottom pieces (Fig. 1). Glue the BL frame together by butting the top and bottom pieces into the side pieces. Place frame faces front-side down on work surface.

2 Glue center pieces to sides and bottoms of respective faces for TR, TL, and C frames (Fig. 2). For BL frame,

---

PROJECT SIZE
12x17⁄8x12 inches

TOOLS
- Wood snips
- Scroll saw

SUPPLIES
- 1⁄4-inch craft plywood: 12x12 inches
- 1⁄8-inch craft plywood: 12x12 inches
- 1⁄4x1-inch basswood*: 8 inches
- 1⁄8x1-inch basswood*: 8 inches
- 1⁄8x3⁄8-inch basswood*: 24 inches
- 1⁄16x1⁄2-inch basswood*: 42 inches
- 1⁄16x1⁄4-inch basswood*: 36 inches
- 1⁄16x1⁄8-inch basswood*: 24 inches
- Glass adhesive
- Sandpaper: 120- and 320-grit
- Wood glue
- DecoArt Americana Satins acrylic paint: soft white #DSA02, powder blue #DSA19 and colonial blue #DSA18
- DecoArt Americana staining medium #DSA32
- Black bullet- and fine-tip permanent marker
- Hanging brackets and wire

* Measurements given are actual, not nominal. Standard nominal lumber will need to be ripped and/or planed to size.

Our family
vacation Memories
'05

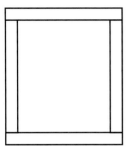

Assemble TR, TL and C frame faces.

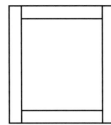

Assemble BL frame face.

Fig. 1

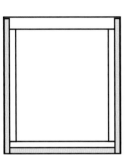

Glue center pieces onto backs of TR, TL and C frame faces.

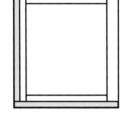

Glue center pieces onto back of BL frame face.

Fig. 2

glue center pieces on the top, bottom and one side of the face. Glue backs to the center pieces of each frame. Let dry.

3 Glue spacers in stacks as follows: four ¼-inch (TR), two ¼-inch and two ⅛-inch (C) and one ¼-inch and one ⅛-inch (BL). Let dry. ***Note:*** *Set the two remaining ⅛-inch spacers aside for later use.*

4 Mix equal parts *colonial blue* and *powder blue*; paint the ¼x12x12-inch piece of craft plywood (frame base), the spacer stacks and all four frames. Let dry.

5 Mix equal parts staining medium and *soft white*; brush onto painted pieces and wipe off with paper towels. Repeat to achieve desired effect. Let dry.

6 Referring to Fig. 3, use glass adhesive to adhere spacers to frame base. Glue the two remaining ⅛-inch spacers on the back of the frame base, each 2 inches from the side and 2 inches from the top.

7 Center and glue each frame onto its respective spacer, taking care that picture openings are at the top for TR, TL, and C frames and to the side for BL frame. Let dry.

8 Personalize the frame collage with the dual-tip marker.

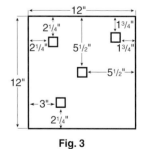

Fig. 3
Adhere spacers to frame base.

9 Attach hanging brackets and wire to the ⅛-inch spacers on the back. ●

STAIRSTEP PICTURE FRAME

Design by Sue Reeves

The stair-step effect draws attention toward a favorite photo—which is right where you want it to be!

CUTTING

1 Rip the oak plywood to 9½ inches wide, then cut into five 11½-inch lengths to make five layer pieces. If using a sampling of several sources, try to keep the top grain on all running the same direction.

2 Measure and mark a border around each of the five layers as follows: 1 inch for frame No. 1 (back), 2 inches for frame No. 2, 1¾ inches for frame No. 3, 1½ inches for frame No. 4 and 1¼ inches for frame No. 5.

3 Drill a pilot hole for the scroll-saw blade on each border outline and cut out center of each frame with scroll saw.

ASSEMBLE

1 Sand the face and edges of each layer; remove dust.

2 Glue and clamp together the back frame No. 1 and frame No. 2 with outer edges flush. Set aside to dry.

3 At the same time, glue and clamp together frame No. 3 and frame No. 4 with outer edges flush. Let dry.

4 Glue and clamp together both glued sections and frame No. 5 with outer edges flush. Let dry.

5 Sand the outer edges, removing excess glue. Remove dust.

6 Spray with two coats of clear polyurethane, allowing to dry after each coat. Sand lightly, remove dust, then apply a third coat and let dry.

7 Attach hanging hardware to back of frame.

8 To use, insert photo in back recess; back with cardboard cut to fit and secure in place with tape. ●

PROJECT SIZE
9½x⅞x11½ inches

TOOLS
- Table saw or circular saw with edge guide
- Drill with bit sized for scroll-saw blade
- Scroll saw
- Clamps

SUPPLIES
- ¼-inch oak plywood: 1x8-foot scrap
- Wood glue
- Clear polyurethane spray finish
- Hanging hardware

A WARM WELCOME

Design by Loretta Mateik

Blooming flowers extend a warm welcome to friends and neighbors.

INSTRUCTIONS

1 Join flower pattern to make full-size pattern; transfer outline onto ¼-inch plywood. Cut with scroll saw. Sand rough edges and wipe clean. Transfer detail lines of flower.

2 Using the table saw, cut ⅜-inch plywood to 8½x10 inches for sign.

3 Base-coat the sign with *toffee*; base-coat the flowers with *country red* and the leaves with a 4:1 mixture of *Hauser medium green* and *titanium white*. Let dry. Lightly sand to knock down raised grain, then wipe clean.

4 Shade-in the petal separations on the flowers with *antique maroon*. Using *Hauser dark green*, shade outside edges of the leaves and center vein lines.

5 Mix enough *sable brown* with *toffee* to slightly darken it. Use this mixture to randomly apply the checkerboard pattern to the sign. Let dry.

6 Position Welcome pattern on sign with top and side edges even; transfer lettering and vertical lines, extending lines the full length of the sign.

7 Paint lettering with *lamp black*. With *sable brown,* shade around outside edges of the sign and paint vertical lines. Let dry.

8 Attach sawtooth hangers to the top back of sign. Glue flower piece to the front of the sign. Erase pattern lines that may still be visible.

9 Apply several light coats of satin varnish, following manufacturer's directions. ●

PROJECT SIZE
10½x⅝x13 inches

TOOLS
- Table saw
- Scroll saw
- Drill with ¹⁄₃₂-inch bit

SUPPLIES
- ⅜-inch plywood: 12x24 inches
- ¼-inch plywood: 8x12 inches
- Sandpaper
- Checkerboard stencil
- DecoArt Americana acrylic paints: toffee #DA059, antique maroon #DA160, Hauser dark green #DA133, sable brown #DA061, Hauser medium green #DA132, lamp black #DA067, country red #DA018 and titanium white #DA01
- DecoArt Americana satin varnish #DS15
- Two 1¾-inch sawtooth hangers

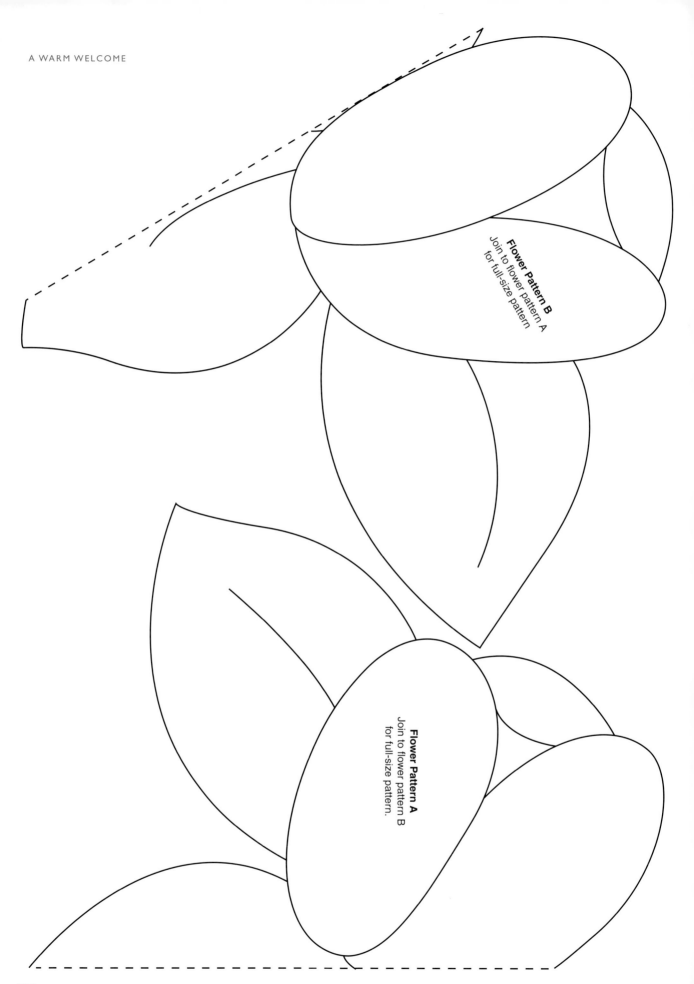

Flower Pattern B
Join to flower pattern A
for full-size pattern

Flower Pattern A
Join to flower pattern B
for full-size pattern.

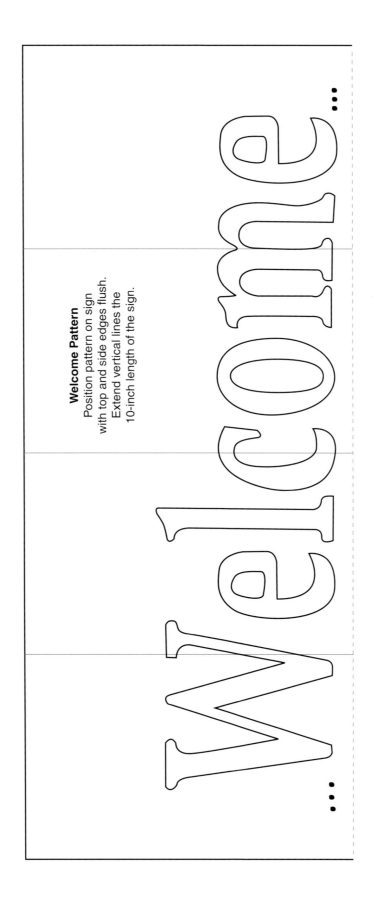

Welcome Pattern
Position pattern on sign with top and side edges flush. Extend vertical lines the 10-inch length of the sign.

HANDS OFF MY CARROT!

Design by Loretta Mateik

This floppy-eared fellow won't be letting go of his dinner any time soon!

INSTRUCTIONS

1 Transfer the pattern outlines for two hands, one nose, one face/arm/carrot and one body to the ⅛-inch plywood. Drill ¹⁄₁₆-inch starter holes in waste areas, then cut out pieces with scroll saw. Drill ¹⁄₃₂-inch holes on face/arm/carrot piece as indicated on pattern. Sand rough edges smooth and wipe clean.

2 Referring to patterns for area separations, base-coat pieces as follows:
Note: Apply multiple coats as needed, letting dry and lightly sanding between each coat.

PROJECT SIZE
2⅞x⅜x3⅛ inches

TOOLS
- Drill with ¹⁄₁₆- and ¹⁄₃₂- inch bits
- Scroll saw
- Wire cutters

SUPPLIES
- ⅛-inch birch plywood: 4x6 inches
- Sandpaper
- 28-gauge black craft wire
- Wood glue

Bunny face/arm/carrot—arm and face, *titanium white*; carrot root, *tangelo orange*; carrot top, *Hauser medium green*.
Body—body, *titanium white*; carrot root, *tangelo orange*; carrot top, *Hauser medium green*.
Nose—*baby pink*.
Hands—*titanium white*.

3 Referring to Fig. 1 and photo, apply pattern detail as follows:
Bunny face/carrot—With *uniform blue*, shade outside edge of face, centers of ears and face/ears, face/carrot and face/arm separations. With

- 1½-inch pin back
- DecoArt Americana acrylic paints: titanium white #DA01, uniform blue #DA086, lamp black #DA067, tangelo orange #DA196, antique maroon #DA160, primary yellow #DA201, baby pink #DA031, Hauser light green #DA131, Hauser dark green #DA133, Hauser medium green #DA132 and country red #DA018
- Matte varnish

antique maroon, shade outside edge of carrot root. With *Hauser dark green*, shade separations of carrot tops, then lightly stipple carrot top. Highlight carrot top by lightly stippling again with *Hauser light green*. Dry-brush center of carrot root with *primary yellow* to highlight. With *lamp black*, draw fine lines on carrot root; paint lines for eyebrows and mouth, and dot eyes on face. Add tiny dots of *titanium white* to eyes for highlights. Apply blush to cheeks very lightly with *country red*.

Body—With *uniform blue*, shade outer edges of feet and body/leg separations. Add highlight marks to feet with *lamp black*.
Nose—Shade lower edge of nose with *antique maroon*; add highlight mark with *titanium white*.
Hands—Shade outer edges with *uniform blue*; add highlight marks with *lamp black*.

4 Cut two 2-inch lengths of black wire. Insert ends through holes in the face from the back for whiskers; cut to desired length.

5 Referring to Fig. 1 and photo, glue face/arm/carrot to body; glue nose to face; glue hands to carrot. Let dry.

6 Glue pin back to back of body; let dry. Seal with several coats of matte varnish. ●

Hand Cut 2

Nose

Body

Fig. 1
Pattern Detail

Drill 1/32"
holes.

X   X

Face/Arm/Carrot
Pattern

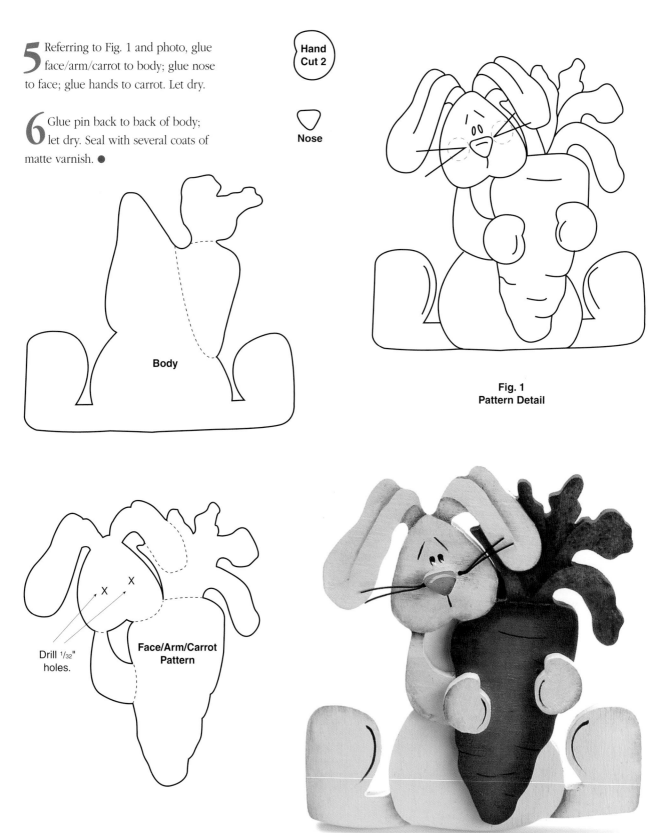

Shown larger than lifesize for painting details

SIMPLE CELEBRATION

Design by Loretta Mateik

Celebrate independence with a scroll-sawn interpretation of Old Glory.

INSTRUCTIONS

1 Using the table saw, rip a 7½-inch-wide piece from the ½x12x12-inch plywood to make the 7½x12-inch flag piece. Transfer flag pattern to flag, extending horizontal stripes the full width of the flag.

2 Use scroll saw to cut out shaded areas between stars, drilling starter holes with 3⁄32-inch bit. Sand rough edges smooth; wipe clean.

3 Base-coat border around stars with *true blue;* paint stars with *titanium white* and alternate stripes with *country red* and *titanium white*. Let dry.

4 Sand lightly and wipe clean. Retouch paint if needed.

5 Set the router V-groove-bit depth to 1⁄16 inch; using an edge guide rout a groove on each stripe line. Shade red stripes with *antique maroon*.

6 Drill 1⁄16-inch pilot holes in top edge of flag, 1 inch from each side; attach the screw eyes. Weave wire through screw eyes several times; wrap end of wire to secure.

7 Erase visible pattern lines; seal with several coats of varnish following manufacturer's instructions. ●

PROJECT SIZE
12x½x7½ inches

TOOLS
- Table saw
- Drill with 1⁄16- and 3⁄32-inch bits
- Scroll saw
- Router with 90-degree ½-inch V-groove bit and edge guide

SUPPLIES
- ½-inch plywood: 12x12 inches
- Sandpaper
- DecoArt Americana acrylic paints: titanium white #DA01, country red #DA018, true blue #DA036 and antique maroon #DA160
- Multipurpose satin varnish
- Two ½-inch eye screws and hanging wire

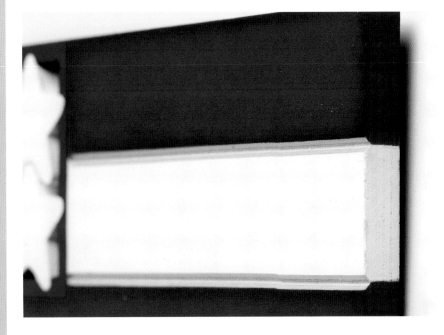

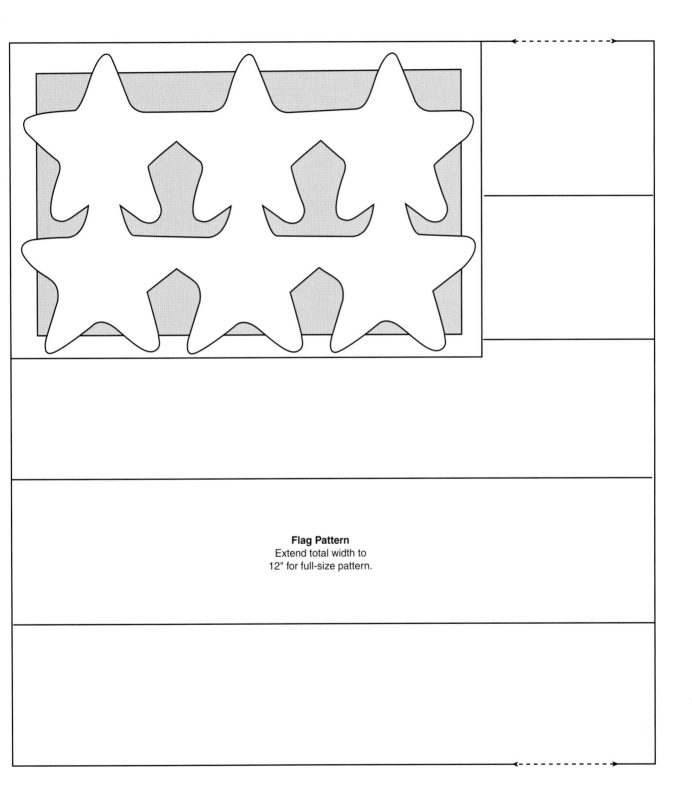

Flag Pattern
Extend total width to
12" for full-size pattern.

BACK-TO-SCHOOL BOOKMARKS

Designs by Loretta Mateik

Head back to the classroom with a half dozen scroll sawn bookmarks in sassy school-yard designs.

CUTTING

1 Cut ⅟₁₆-inch birch plywood in half to make two 12x4-inch pieces. Cut each of the 12x4-inch pieces into three 4x4-inch pieces.

2 Transfer the outline of the bookmark pattern onto one 4x4-inch piece of birch plywood. **Note:** *Because of the thinness of the wood, it will be easiest to cut at least three of the same design at one time by layering pieces and taping together with double-sided tape. Remove tape after cutting.*

Drill ⅟₁₆-inch starter holes as indicated on the pattern, then thread the scroll saw blade through the hole and cut out the pattern.

3 Carefully sand smooth and wipe clean. **Note:** *For ease in sanding small areas, wrap sandpaper around a toothpick.*

BASE-COATING

Note: *Apply multiple coats as needed. Let dry and lightly sand between coats.*

1 Base-coat both sides of each paper clip portion with *shimmering silver.*

2 Base-coat the top portion of each bookmark as follows:
Apple—*country red* with *dark chocolate* stem
Worm—*Hauser light green*
Ruler—*antique white*
Book—*lamp black*
Globe—*Prussian blue*
School Bus—*primary yellow* with *lamp black* wheels

PAINT DETAILING

Note: *Black fine-tip permanent marker may be used instead of lamp black to add fine lines and dots.*

1 Transfer detail lines to each bookmark and paint as follows:
Apple—Shade outside edge of apple with *antique maroon*; dry-brush *primary yellow* on center of apple to highlight.
Worm—Shade body segments with *Hauser dark green*. With *lamp black*, apply a tiny dot for eye; draw a fine line for eyebrow. Apply *country red* for cheek. Highlight the eye with a dot of *titanium white*.

PROJECT SIZE
Approximately 1x⅟₁₆x3 inches each

TOOLS
- Scroll saw
- Drill with ⅟₁₆-inch bit

SUPPLIES
- ⅟₁₆-inch birch plywood: 12x8 inches*
- Double-sided tape (optional)
- Sandpaper
- DecoArt Dazzling Metallics: shimmering silver #DA070
- DecoArt Americana acrylic paints: country red #DA018, antique maroon #DA160, primary yellow #DA201, dark chocolate #DA065, Hauser light green #DA131, Hauser dark green #DA133, lamp black #DA067, antique white #DA058, titanium white #DA01, Hauser medium green #DA132, Prussian blue #DA138 and burnt sienna #DA063
- Black fine-tip permanent marker (optional)
- Matte varnish

* Materials given are sufficient to make six bookmarks.

Ruler—Line message and markings with *lamp black*. Shade outside edge with *dark chocolate*.

Book—With *titanium white*, use a fine-tip brush to paint line down left side of book, then lightly stipple area on right side of line and let dry; paint label and let dry. Line book title on label with *lamp black*.

Globe—Shade outside edge with *Prussian blue*; shade land mass areas with *Hauser medium green*.

School Bus—With *titanium white*, paint windows, doors and bumpers; dot wheel centers. With *lamp black*, outline windows and doors and draw lines on bus. Shade outer edges of *primary yellow* portion with *burnt sienna*. ●

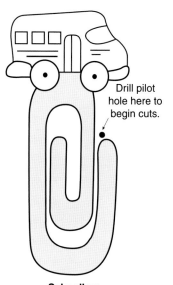

Schoolbus Bookmark

Drill pilot hole here to begin cuts.

Bookworm Bookmark

Drill pilot hole here to begin cuts.

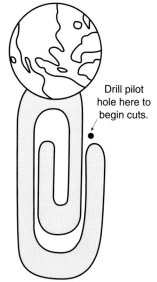

Globe Bookmark

Drill pilot hole here to begin cuts.

Math
101

Math Bookmark

Drill pilot hole here to begin cuts.

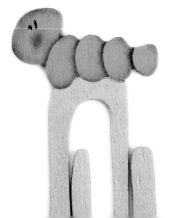

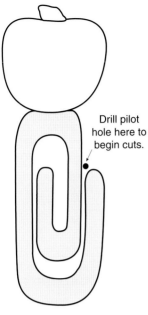

Apple Bookmark

Drill pilot hole here to begin cuts.

Teachers Rule

Teacher Bookmark

Drill pilot hole here to begin cuts.

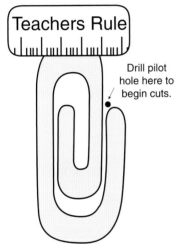

ABC TRAY PUZZLE

Design by Anna Thompson

Little ones can learn their letters and have fun at the same time!

INSTRUCTIONS

1 Attach the pattern to the ⅜-inch Baltic birch with spray adhesive, leaving an even border on all sides. Drill ¹⁄₁₆-inch holes as indicated on pattern.

2 Carefully cut out the inside shapes only of letters A, B, D, O, P, Q, and R, reserving cut-out pieces for later use. Carefully cut out the rest of the letters and set aside. *Note: For the letters on the ends, the saw may have to be turned off in order to maneuver the board to finish the cuts.*

3 Spread white wood glue sparingly on the back of the ⅜-inch plywood. Set it on the ¼-inch plywood, making all edges flush. Weight or clamp together and let glue dry.

4 Glue the letter inserts in place by first placing their respective letters in place, then brushing a slight amount of glue on the back of the inserts and setting in place. Make sure there is no squeeze out and that none of the surrounding letters are inadvertently glued down.

5 Using 150-grit sandpaper, sand the outer edges of the tray smooth and flush. Set all the letters in place and sand off the paper template. Remove letters and sand edges.

6 Spray a coat of lacquer over the face, back and edges of puzzle tray and each letter. Let dry; sand lightly with 220-grit sandpaper.

7 Paint the tops of the letters as desired, using paint markers. ●

PROJECT SIZE
16x⅝x11 inches

TOOLS
- Drill with ¹⁄₁₆-inch bit
- Scroll saw with #4 blade
- Heavy weight or clamps
- Sander with 150- and 220-grit sandpaper

SUPPLIES
- ⅜-inch Baltic birch plywood: 11x16 inches
- ¼-inch Baltic birch plywood: 11x16 inches
- Spray adhesive
- White wood glue
- Paint markers in assorted colors
- Clear spray lacquer

Left Alphabet Layout
Join to right pattern layout
for full-size pattern.
Enlarge 125%.

Right Alphabet Layout
Join to left pattern layout
for full-size pattern.
Enlarge 125%.

POSTCARD PUZZLES

Design by Anna Thompson

A wide variety of scrapbook papers makes it easy to create a custom puzzle for everyone on your list.

INSTRUCTIONS (FOR EACH PUZZLE)

1 Cut the ⅛-inch birch plywood to 5⅛x7 inches. With spray adhesive, attach the scrapbook papers to the plywood.

2 Using stencil tape, tape puzzle pattern over the papered plywood; tape the card stock to the bottom of the plywood.

3 Cut the puzzle pieces following the jigsaw pattern. *Note: Keep the piece moving through the saw blade for smooth lines.*

4 Gently remove the tape; reglue any lifted areas of paper. ●

PROJECT SIZE
7x⅛x5⅛ inches

TOOLS
■ Scroll saw with #2 blade

SUPPLIES
■ ⅛-inch Baltic birch plywood: 8x16 inches
■ Spray adhesive
■ Two 5⅛x7-inch pieces of scrapbook paper in contrasting patterns
■ 5⅛x7-inch piece card stock
■ Stencil tape

SAWING TIPS
• Make yourself comfortable. If you will be sawing for a while, sit down.
• Tension and saw speed are critical factors in scroll saw blade use and longevity. Apply enough tension to hold the blade with no more than ⅛-inch flex from side to side. Too much can snap the blade; not enough allows for too much flex.
• If using a variable-speed saw, experiment with the speed; 1200–1400 strokes per minute are recommended.
• Blade thickness will depend on the project. Check to make sure the front of the blade has teeth pointing down and to the front.
• Let the saw do the work. Guide, but don't force the wood through.

Puzzle Pattern

FRETWORK
KEEPSAKE BOOK

Design by Anna Thompson

An intricate Pennsylvania Dutch design adorns the cover of a memory book.

INSTRUCTIONS

1 Referring to cutting chart, cut three 8½x11-inch pieces from ⅛-inch birch plywood.

2 Join fretwork patterns for full-size pattern; transfer pattern onto the front of one of the 8½x11-inch plywood pieces. **Note:** *Center pattern on plywood so there is an even border all around cut-out design.*

3 Drill holes for each of the flower centers; drill starter holes in cut-out areas for scroll saw blade, then cut out shaded areas with scroll saw. Using paint markers and referring to photo, paint as desired. Let dry.

4 Paint both sides and all edges of a second 8½x11-inch piece with *flat black* for background; let dry.

PROJECT SIZE
8½x⅜x11 inches

TOOLS
- Table saw
- Drill with ⅛- and ¼-inch drill bits
- Scroll saw

SUPPLIES
- ⅛-inch Baltic birch plywood: 18x24 inches
- Wood glue
- Paint markers
- Flat black paint
- Three 1-inch binder rings

Fretwork Top
Join to fretwork bottom for full-size pattern.
Cut out shaded areas.

Join this edge to fretwork bottom.

5 Glue background to back of cut-out piece with outside edges flush for front cover. Clamp, remove any excess glue immediately and let dry.

6 Stack front cover and last 8½x11-inch piece together; drill three ¼-inch holes centered 5/16-inch from the back edge and at ¾, 5½ and 10¼ inches from the top. Insert binder rings and keepsake pages. ●

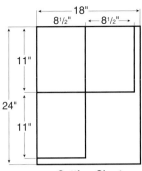

Cutting Chart

Join this edge to fretwork top.

Fretwork Bottom
Join to fretwork top for full-size pattern.
Cut out shaded areas.

ALL ABOUT PLYWOOD

It's lighter in weight, stronger and more stable than solid wood.

Plywood is a building material that is most commonly used in the United States, China and Japan. It is made from layers of thinly sliced wood, or plies, which are glued together under pressure. Each ply is arranged so that the direction of the grain runs perpendicular to the grain in the ply above or below it. This arrangement produces a lightweight but strong, stable building material that won't shrink, twist or warp like solid wood. A relatively recent addition to the plywood family is bendable plywood, or wiggle board. The plies in bendable plywood are glued with the grain running in the same direction. This produces the same lightweight, stable building material, but it bends along the grain without breaking, making it easy to create curved forms.

Plywood is made from different species, depending on its intended use. Softwood plywood is normally made from various combinations of spruce, pine and fir and is typically used in construction and industry. Decorative plywood is faced with hardwoods such as oak, birch, maple, cherry and is well-suited for furniture or in applications where a lightweight yet attractive material is needed. Lauan plywood is made from a group of tree species found in the rain forests of Malaysia and Indonesia. Lauan is used extensively in Japan for concrete forms and inexpensive furniture and is often discarded after only a few years.

The standard size for a sheet of plywood is 4 x 8 feet. In the United States, the most common thicknesses are ¼ to ¾ inches thick depending on how the plywood will be used. Roof sheathing can be as thin as ⅜ inch, while floorboards should be at least ⅝ inch thick, depending on the distance between the floor joists.

In addition to choosing what species and thickness of plywood to use for a project, one must also decide where the project will be used. Interior plywood is made with glues that have limited resistance to water, so projects made with interior plywood should remain inside or in a sheltered area. Exterior plywood is designed to withstand moisture and humid conditions. If a project is going to be exposed to extended periods of moisture, consider using marine-grade plywood. This plywood is made with waterproof glues and is generally used in boat building.

There are several steps involved in the manufacture of plywood. First, logs are selected that are relatively straight and round, free from knots and with minimal decay. The bark is removed from the logs and the logs are steamed to soften the wood. Next, a long knife peels off a thin layer of wood in one continuous strip. The strip is then cut into sheets, stacked and dried to a moisture content of between 6 and 14 percent. Adhesive is applied to the sheets and they are pressed, trimmed

to final size, sanded and graded for quality before being shipped to the local lumberyard.

The earliest known plywood has been dated to about 3500 B.C. in ancient Egypt, where wooden items were made from glued-together veneers. Modern plywood, where the veneer is peeled in one continuous strip, was invented by Emmanuel Nobel, father of Nobel Prize founder Alfred Nobel, in the United States in the mid-19th century.

PLYWOOD TRIVIA

■ Prototype plywood panels for the 1905 World's Fair in Portland, Ore., were produced one at a time, clamped with house jacks and held together with animal glue that smelled so foul, workers had to leave the mill frequently for fresh air breaks.

■ A two-foot-diameter log can be reduced to 400 feet of ¹⁄₁₀-inch veneer in about 15 seconds.

■ The amount of wood remaining after a log has been peeled is about the diameter of a broomstick.

■ Hollywood set builders used to go through a quarter of a million sheets of lauan plywood a year. Some studios have switched to more ecologically sound substitutes for this endangered hardwood, while others have cut back their use.

CONVERSION CHARTS

Standard Lumber Dimensions

NOMINAL	ACTUAL	METRIC
1" x 2"	¾" x 1½"	19 x 38 mm
1" x 3"	¾" x 2½"	19 x 64 mm
1" x 4"	¾" x 3½"	19 x 89 mm
1" x 5"	¾" x 4½"	19 x 114 mm
1" x 6"	¾" x 5½"	19 x 140 mm
1" x 7"	¾" x 6¼"	19 x 159 mm
1" x 8"	¾" x 7¼"	19 x 184 mm
1" x 10"	¾" x 9¼"	19 x 235 mm
1" x 12"	¾" x 11¼"	19 x 286 mm
1¼" x 4"	1" x 3½"	25 x 89 mm
1¼" x 6"	1" x 5½"	25 x 140 mm
1¼" x 8"	1" x 7¼"	25 x 184 mm
1¼" x 10"	1" x 9¼"	25 x 235 mm
1¼" x 12"	1" x 11¼"	25 x 286 mm
1½" x 4"	1¼" x 3½"	32 x 89 mm
1½" x 6"	1¼" x 5½"	32 x 140 mm
1½" x 8"	1¼" x 7¼"	32 x 184 mm
1½" x 10"	1¼" x 9¼"	32 x 235 mm
1½" x 12"	1¼" x 11¼"	32 x 286 mm
2" x 3"	1½" x 2½"	38 x 64 mm
2" x 4"	1½" x 3½"	38 x 89 mm
2" x 6"	1½" x 5½"	38 x 140 mm
2" x 8"	1½" x 7¼"	38 x 184 mm
2" x 10"	1½" x 9¼"	38 x 235 mm
2" x 12"	1½" x 11¼"	38 x 286 mm
3" x 6"	2½" x 5½"	64 x 140 mm
4" x 4"	3½" x 3½"	89 x 89 mm
4" x 6"	3½" x 5½"	89 x 140 mm

Metric Conversions

U.S. MEASUREMENT		MULTIPLIED BY		METRIC MEASUREMENT
Yards	x	.9144	=	Meters (m)
Yards	x	91.44	=	Centimeters (cm)
Inches	x	2.54	=	Centimeters (cm)
Inches	x	25.40	=	Millimeters (mm)
Inches	x	.0254	=	Meters (m)
METRIC MEASUREMENT		**MULTIPLIED BY METRIC MEASUREMENT**		
Centimeters	x	.3937	=	Inches
Meters	x	1.0936	=	Yards

SPECIAL THANKS

We thank the talented woodworking designers whose work is featured in this collection.

Barbara Greve
Cheery Children's Bench 97
Corner Curio Shelf 31
Handy Rack 28
Memories Collage 145
Oriental Storage Nook 14
Petite Pastel Table 94
Portable Box Mirror 128
Scrolls & Swirls Desk Set 131
Simple Porch Planter 87

Angie Kopacek
Simply CDs 42

Loretta Mateik
A Warm Welcome 150
Back-To-School Bookmarks 160
Checkerboard Flower Table 90
Hands off My Carrot! 157
Petite Pie Cabinet 37
Simple Celebration 154
Sweet Jelly Cabinet 24
Trinket Catch-All 106

Amy Phillips
Bedside Bookcase 67
Easy Room Divider 70

Sue Reeves
Stairstep Display Ledge 134
Stairstep Picture Frame 148

Delores F. Ruzicka
Cattail Shadows 140

Patti J. Ryan
Message & Mail Center 34
Seaside Cooler 82
Six-Drawer Clock 114
Summer Cottage Curio 78
Versatile Display Shelf 136
Wiggle-Board Clock 119

Annellen & Alex Simpkins
Parquet-Tray 109

Anna Thompson
ABC Tray Puzzle 164
Cherry Kitchen Base Cabinet 45
Cherry Kitchen Upper
    Cabinet 53
Easy Rolling Garden Cart 73
Fretwork Keepsake Book 171
Office in an Armoire 58
Plywood Perfect 6
Postcard Puzzles 168

Linda Van Gehuchten
Curvaceous Plywood Bowl 100
Rainbow Ring Holder 122
Simply Plywood
    Ring Holder 125
Twist & Turned Plywood
    Bowl 103
Two-Tone Side Table 18